A GUERNSEYMAN GOES TO WAR

PRIVATE LATIMER LE POIDEVIN'S NOTEBOOK, 1917-1919

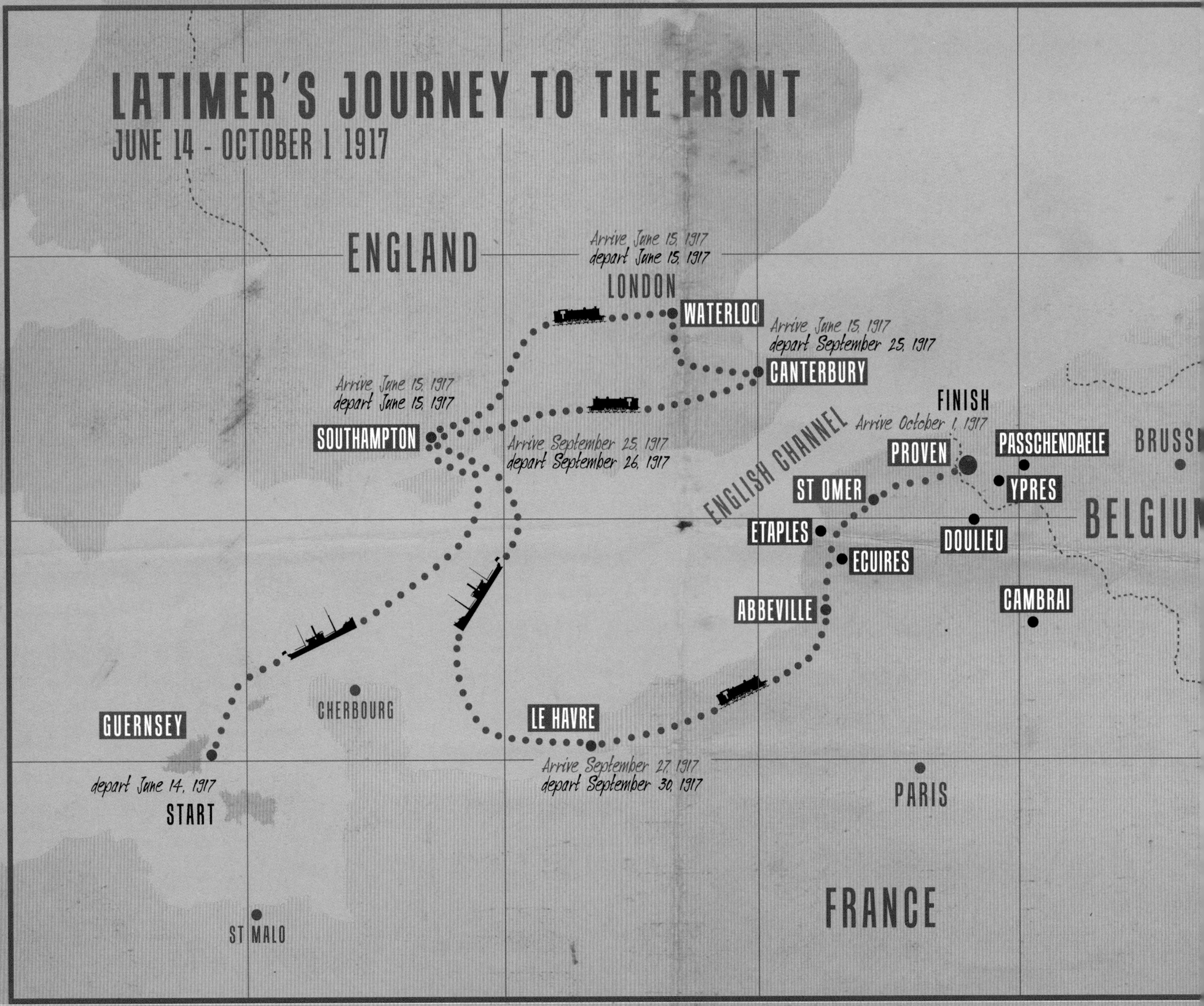

LATIMER'S JOURNEY TO THE FRONT
JUNE 14 - OCTOBER 1 1917

ENGLAND

Arrive June 15, 1917
depart June 15, 1917

LONDON

WATERLOO

Arrive June 15, 1917
depart September 25, 1917

CANTERBURY

Arrive June 15, 1917
depart June 15, 1917

SOUTHAMPTON

Arrive September 25, 1917
depart September 26, 1917

FINISH

Arrive October 1, 1917

PROVEN

PASSCHENDAELE

BRUSS

ENGLISH CHANNEL

ST OMER

YPRES

BELGIUM

ETAPLES

DOULIEU

ECUIRES

ABBEVILLE

CAMBRAI

GUERNSEY

CHERBOURG

LE HAVRE

depart June 14, 1917

START

Arrive September 27, 1917
depart September 30, 1917

PARIS

FRANCE

ST MALO

A GUERNSEYMAN GOES TO WAR
PRIVATE LATIMER LE POIDEVIN'S NOTEBOOK, 1917-1919

NETHERLANDS

GERMANY

LUXEMBOURG

CONTENTS

656 Private Latimer Le Poidevin served with the Royal Guernsey Light Infantry (RGLI) between January 1917 and June 1919. According to his family on his return to Guernsey after demobilisation he made notes of his experiences in a small notebook which he put away and never referred to again.

This book is based on that notebook. The original is thought to still be in the possession of his descendants but could not be found in 2006 when the current project was started. However Major Edwin Parks had a photocopy made during the compilation of his book *Diex Aix: God Help Us, the Guernseymen Who Marched Away, 1914-1918.*[1] A literal transcription was made from this copy, and this was then altered where necessary into a more readable form of English. Private Le Poidevin like many of his contemporaries spoke Guernsey French, an old Norman form of the language as his first language, but when writing he used English, which was the

656 PRIVATE LATIMER LE POIDEVIN

language he learnt at school. This means that the original document though written in English contained many grammatical constructions and expressions based on Guernsey French. This made it more difficult for a contemporary reader to follow so small changes have been made in the interests of clarity, though efforts were made to retain the 'feel' of the original.

Events described in the notebook were compared with primary sources such as the RGLI War Diaries, Casualty Lists and Movement Orders in order to check the accuracy of Latimer's account. This comparison also showed how official records translated into individual experience. The two sources matched very closely, showing that his recollection of events was surprisingly accurate in view of the turmoil of the times. It is likely that he jotted down notes of some form during the War, given the number of dates and place-names he

quotes. Accounts from secondary sources that provide the reader with a wider view of events were added in order to place one conscript's view within the context of major events of the period.

Detailed appendices created for this book have been placed on the website www. greatwarci.net. They consist of annotated Battalion Casualty Lists matched with events described in each chapter of the book, and are referred to where appropriate within the text. Anyone wishing to find out more about family members who fought with the RGLI might find it useful to check the website. General information can be found under War on Land/Guernsey. Information on men who died is listed under Casualties of War/Bailiwick of Guernsey/ RoH Online Search. Those who served and survived are included under RoS/Online Search. We are always pleased to hear from anyone who can add further information.

AUTHOR'S NOTES

Sections in italics were transcribed from Private Le Poidevin's notebook. Those in plain text are my notes based on sources such as the official War Diary of the 1st (Service) Battalion, Royal Guernsey Light Infantry, Movement Orders, Relief Orders, Order of Battle and the official Casualty Lists, held in the National Archives as documents W/O 95-2302. Reference has also been made to Parks (1992)[2] and other military histories which are annotated as endnotes. Any errors are entirely down to me and comments can be made on the website.

INTRODUCTION

ACKNOWLEDGEMENTS

In the course of compiling this book I have had help from many people. I would first like to thank members of the Le Poidevin family (my 'cousins'), especially Mrs Doreen Hall and her son Ian for allowing me to use the notebook, providing a photograph of Latimer and helping with family history aspects. Thanks are also due to Major Edwin Parks for alerting me to the existence of the notebook and for the use of material in his own book *Diex Aix*, also for his comments on various military matters. Roger Frisby assisted with checking the transcription of the notebook and put the appendices online at www.greatwarci.net. Mark Bougourd made his compilations of the RGLI Nominal Rolls available and helped with medal citations, Paul Dorey allowed me use of transcriptions of the Battalion War Diary, Movement Orders, Relief Orders and Casualty Lists. The staff of Guernsey Museums & Galleries (especially Matt. Harvey) and the Priaulx Library gave me access to various source materials, for which many thanks. Special thanks go to the members of the Channel Islands Great War Study Group especially our founder Barrie Bertram and Jersey member Ian Ronayne for their continued support and encouragement and to Kay Lane for her first proof reading and comments. The book has been edited by Jason Monaghan.

Finally I wish to pay my respects to all the brave men and women of the Bailiwick whose lives were affected by the Great War. The changes that it brought about altered their lives in irreversible ways, and there cannot have been a family that was not touched to some extent by the events of those years.

Liz Walton

ABBREVIATIONS

The abbreviations used in this book and the online appendices comply where possible with standard forms and also with those used in Parks.[3] Battalion Casualty Lists sometimes show men as missing on a certain date. Where evidence from other sources such as Commonwealth War Graves Commission records adds further information, it is also listed. For example a man might be listed as Missing, Wnds, DOW. This would mean that when the records were made he was missing but it was later found that he had been wounded and then died as a result of his injuries. Any discrepancies are mentioned in endnotes to the online appendices.

BRCS	*British Red Cross*
Capt.	*Captain*
Cpl	*Corporal*
CSM	*Company Sergeant Major*
CWGC	*Commonwealth War Graves Commission*
DB	*Silver discharge badge awarded*
DCM	*Distinguished Conduct Medal awarded*
DGMS	*Director General Medical Services*
DOW	*Died of wounds*
Gas	*Victim of poison gas*
GSW	*Gunshot wounds*
IES	*Invalided to England because of illness*
IEW	*Invalided to England wounded*
KIA	*Killed in action*
L/Cpl	*Lance-Corporal*
Lt	*Lieutenant*
MC	*Military Cross awarded*
MM	*Military Medal awarded*
NCO	*Non-commissioned officer*
PH	*Phenate Hexamine [Helmet] (hooded gas mask)*
POW	*Prisoner of war*
Pte	*Private*
QMS	*Quarter Master Sergeant*
RGLI	*Royal Guernsey Light Infantry*
RIF	*Royal Irish Fusiliers*
RIR	*Royal Irish Regiment*
Sgt	*Sergeant*
TE	*Sent back to England, reason unknown*
Wnds	*Wounded*

NOTES ON MAPS

A series of simplified maps are included in this book. Symbols are used throughout as detailed below:

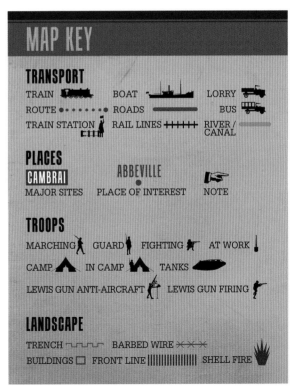

MAP KEY

TRANSPORT
TRAIN   BOAT   LORRY
ROUTE   ROADS   BUS
TRAIN STATION   RAIL LINES   RIVER / CANAL

PLACES
CAMBRAI   ABBEVILLE   NOTE
MAJOR SITES   PLACE OF INTEREST

TROOPS
MARCHING   GUARD   FIGHTING   AT WORK
CAMP   IN CAMP   TANKS
LEWIS GUN ANTI-AIRCRAFT   LEWIS GUN FIRING

LANDSCAPE
TRENCH   BARBED WIRE
BUILDINGS   FRONT LINE   SHELL FIRE

LATIMER
AND HIS FAMILY

Had he been born at any other period in Guernsey's history, Latimer Thomas Le Poidevin (pronounced Le Ped-vin) is unlikely to have ever gone to war in a foreign country. He was born in Guernsey on the 31st of January 1892 the elder son of islander Thomas John Le Poidevin and his wife Annie, née Simkins, of Southampton. Thomas, like many other Guernseymen of the time, was a grower. He had worked as a gardener at Saumarez Park before becoming involved in the family horticultural business at Les Orgeries, Pleinheaume Road in the Vale, where they grew fruit and vegetables for export. Thomas and Annie's family consisted of Latimer, his younger brother Herbert, and four daughters: Annie, Elsie, Irene and Ruth.

Latimer was 19 years old when he married Alice Mary Allez on the 27th of January 1911 at St Saviour's Church in Guernsey. By the time he was called up in 1917 he had a daughter Dorothy, age 6 and a son Latimer, age 5. His brother Herbert, who was some six years younger,

married Alice Mary Mauger at St Sampson's Church on the 24th of February 1917, soon after being called up. He left the island just over six months later. Both brothers were born and educated in Guernsey and like many islanders in those pre-war years had rarely if ever left the island. They left school in their early teens and were then employed as agricultural and horticultural labourers in the family's greenhouses and on relatives' farms.

THE GUERNSEY MILITIA

One part of island life that the Le Poidevin brothers would both have participated in was Militia training. This was compulsory for all fit male inhabitants between the ages of 16 and 60, "à l'exception de ceux qui par la Constitution et l'usage de cette île en sont exemptes".

The Militia was a uniformed military force composed of civilians whose role was to supplement the regular army in times of emergency. It had existed in some form since the fourteenth century. In 1914 the Guernsey Militia consisted of two Light Infantry Battalions, the first recruited in the 'town' (St Peter Port), and the second from the 'country' parishes making up the rest of the island. New recruits had three weeks of training, and after completing their term with the Battalion, where they had to complete an annual camp, were placed in reserve. Some islanders served in the Royal Guernsey Artillery and Engineers (RGA& E) which consisted of the Royal Guernsey Artillery, two Engineer companies and a Field Artillery company.

left
Grapes being grown in a large wood and glass 'greenhouse'. Guernsey, circa 1900-1915.
GUEMG 2006.9.13c. © Guernsey Museum.

above
Men of the Royal Guernsey Artillery with 2 field guns and limbers. Les Beaucamps, Guernsey. Circa 1910-1914.
© Guernsey Museum.

ALDERNEY

In Alderney things were slightly different.[4] Their Militia, the Royal Alderney Artillery and Engineers was there to supplement the regular army garrison based on the island. Young men could volunteer for service with the Militia at the age of 16. If there were not enough volunteers, a ballot was held. The authorities would say that there was a need for so many men and names would be picked at random. New recruits trained for 21 days at Fort Tourgis. Then the old hands or 'Effectives' were called up for 11 days and the recruits trained with them. After this they also classed as Effectives, training for eleven days a year for nine years. At the end of this time they joined the Reserves where they remained until they were 45 years old. Two and a half days of training each year were set aside for rifle and artillery practice. Kit and rifles were stored in the Militia Arsenal in Ollivier Street, while a Battery of field guns was kept in the sheds at the Butes Arsenal.

There was also a Cadet Company made up of boys from Elizabeth College, a boys public school in St Peter Port. The Cadet Company was later detached from the RGA&E to become an Officer Training Corps. Thus all young, fit males in the Bailiwick undertook some form of military training.

THE THREAT OF
WAR GROWS

As the threat of war in Europe grew, the Guernsey authorities decided to intensify Militia training so that by 1914, they were "as highly trained as any peacetime part-time force could be."[5] They were mobilised as soon as it became evident that war would be declared. A special edition of the *Gazette de Guernesey*, the island's official newspaper was printed on Thursday 30th July 1914. It carried the "General Order Embodying the Royal Militia of Guernsey", and was printed in both French and English so that there could be no misunderstanding whichever language islanders spoke.

The Order stated that "Whereas by article 9 of the Ordinance relating to Royal Militia of the Island of Guernsey....it is provided that, in certain special circumstances, the States of the island of Guernsey shall furnish a contingent of Militia consisting of 2,000 non-commissioned officers and men, to be embodied for such period of active service as shall be prescribed by Royal Proclamation or by General Order of the Lieutenant Governor, and whereas in my opinion such special circumstances have arisen; now therefore in pursuance of the said Ordinance I do hereby order that 1,000 non-commissioned officers and men, Effectives of the said contingent of Militia, be forthwith embodied from this date until further orders, and further that the remainder of the above said contingent, viz: 1,000 men of Section "A" of the Reserve, be prepared to join their respective Regiments when called upon".

It was signed by H.M. Lawson, Major-General, Lieutenant Governor and General Officer commanding the Troops in the Island of Guernsey and its Dependencies.

above
Major-General Henry Merrick Lawson, Lieutenant-Governor of Guernsey.
Guernsey Weekly Press, Saturday 21st March 1914.

left
The Elizabeth College Cadet Company Shooting Team. 1915.
GMAG 2007.32. © Guernsey Museum.

Detail of The Artillery Barracks, Guernsey - from Clarence Battery.
Colour Lithographic Print published by M. Moss, 1829.
GUELI GMAG 1340 L. © Guernsey Museum.

THE WAR
BEGINS

The British Army had for many years maintained a Garrison at Fort George in St Peter Port, and the 2nd Battalion the Yorkshire Regiment (the Green Howards) were stationed there at the end of July 1914. When war broke out they were called back to England initially but were soon to form part of the first British Expeditionary Force in France and Flanders. According to local newspapers they marched to the White Rock (the main passenger departure point at St Peter Port harbour) clad in "unfamiliar" khaki rather than their usual scarlet uniforms where they were given an enthusiastic send off. The Militia had been mobilized to take over from these regular army soldiers in the first instance but a large contingent from the 4th (Reserve) Battalion, North Staffordshire Regiment soon arrived to take their place. This was a Home Battalion, consisting of men who were as yet untrained or were not likely to be fit for active service overseas. Reports in the *Guernsey Evening Press* stated that they appeared to have come "direct from the mines and potteries of the Midlands" without uniform or arms, a far cry from the smart turnout and dress uniforms of the Green Howards and other regiments stationed on the island before the war. They took up residence at Fort George, but the accommodation was insufficient for the number of men that arrived so they had to build a "canvas city" on the Fort Field for the early part of their stay.

THE ISLANDS REACT

First Class Soldier L. FLEURY, a French Reservist, who before the outbreak of the War was in the employ of Mr. Ozanne, Lilyvale, and resided at Hougue du Pommier, Castel.

left
A French Reservist recalled to active service.
Guernsey Weekly Press, 1914.

below
Plans for a defensive fire trench and machine gun position at Rocq(u)aine, Guernsey. 16th February 1916.
W078/4398. © The National Archives, Kew.

In Alderney[6] rockets were fired from Fort Albert as a signal to the regular army men to report back to their barracks. Militiamen were summoned by ringing the church bells and Reservists were also mobilised. Militia gunners took over the manning of the two 12 pounders and two 6 inch guns at the Cavalier Battery in Fort Albert from the 17th Company, Royal Garrison Artillery while the Militia Engineers took over from the regular Royal Engineers at Grosnez.

The "purely precautionary" mobilisation of the Militia across the Bailiwick was to last from the summer of 1914 until late 1916. During the first part of this period the men lived in camp and underwent regular training, they patrolled the cliffs and erected fortifications at bays such as L'Ancresse which it was felt might be the target for enemy landings. Barbed wire fencing, machine gun emplacements and trenches were constructed at various bays along the west coast to protect the island from invaders. However this intense activity only lasted for a few months. Under normal conditions much of the Bailiwick's agricultural labour force consisted of migrant labourers from rural areas of Brittany and Normandy where there was high unemployment. The French system of National Service however conscripted all fit young men into full time service with the armed forces for a couple of years.

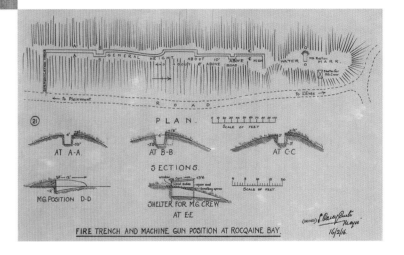

FIRE TRENCH AND MACHINE GUN POSITION AT ROCQAINE BAY.

After this they were placed in reserve until well into their middle years. All French Reservists, including those living overseas were recalled to fight for their country as soon as war broke out, leaving the Bailiwick without these essential workers. The Lieutenant Governor met with the Bailiff and the Jurats of the Royal Court on February 14th 1915 to discuss the problem of the labour shortage, and it was decided that in future Militia Reservists would only be called up once a month, and some men would be released to follow their normal occupations. Men were also released from military duties to work on the farms at harvest time.

THE FIRST
VOLUNTEERS

Local newspapers show that as soon as war broke out, many Guernseymen had volunteered to join the British Army, which was an all-volunteer force at this stage. The need for men to join the "New Army" intensified, however, so early in 1915 the States offered to send an Infantry Company and an Artillery Ammunition Column to join the war effort. Both consisted of volunteers from the local force. The infantrymen eventually formed two companies, one in the 6th Battalion the Royal Irish Regiment (RIR), where they formed "D" Company and the Machine Gun Section. Some later drafts went to the 3rd Battalion RIR, a reserve Battalion for the 6th, but they were later transferred to the 7th Battalion, the Royal Irish Fusiliers (RIF). Some also went straight to 7 RIF.

right
Men of the Guernsey and Alderney Royal Guernsey Artillery Regiments forming the 9th Divisional Ammunition Column. On board ship departing St. Peter Port Harbour. May 1915.
GMAG 1985.169. © Guernsey Museum.

left
The Guernsey Contingent of the Royal Irish Regiment marching through St. Peter Port on their way to the harbour. March 1915.
GMAG 1991.112. © Guernsey Museum.

THE FIRST
CASUALTIES

A third group of volunteers consisting of the Officers and men of the Royal Guernsey Artillery and Engineers formed the 9th Divisional Ammunition Column. They went first to Salisbury Plain for training then proceeded to France in May 1915.

The first Infantry contingent left the island to join the Irish regiments in March 1915, and was soon followed by several more drafts. After training in England and Ireland they went to France in December 1915, where they were attached to units already experienced in trench warfare. More than 90 of these men, all volunteers, died whilst on active service in France and Flanders between March 1916 and September 1917. Local volunteers also fought with other units and in all branches of the armed services, and many were killed or wounded in the course of the war.

As casualty numbers escalated and the war showed no sign of coming to an end,

Britain's need for more men at the battlefronts increased. In Guernsey General Sir Reginald Hart, V.C., K.C.B., K.C.V.O. had replaced Major General Lawson as the island's Lieutenant Governor in November 1914. Hart was an ardent patriot who had won many awards for bravery, including the Victoria Cross which he was awarded during the second Afghan War.

He was already sixty-six years old when he took up the post of Lieutenant Governor, a role often seen as a reward at the end of a distinguished military career. He soon began to put pressure on the States of Guernsey to introduce conscription in to the Bailiwick. The "Bill for the Compulsory Attestation of Single Men" had been introduced on the British mainland by Prime Minister Asquith on the 6th of January 1916, with the proviso that "... the bill would prove to be a dead letter if the men would come in now of their own free will, for the group system was reopened and the military authorities would continue to

allow them to attest under it."[7] The group system was the scheme that led to the formation of "Pals" battalions consisting of groups of workmates, neighbours, sportsmen etc. who joined up together and stayed together in the same Battalion. The proposed Compulsory Attestation Bill stated that single men or childless widowers who were of military age and had no grounds for exemption were to be treated as though they had attested for enlistment for the period of the war.

Newspaper reports of various speeches that Hart made at public events in Guernsey in 1916 show that he felt that that there were too many "shirkers" in the Bailiwick. This was despite the fact that the proportion of volunteers, though dropping, was still high compared with the national average and that more than 550 local men had already given their lives by the end of 1916.

above
A selection of the Guernsey men reported injured or killed in British Regiments.
Guernsey Weekly Press, 1914-1915.

left
General Sir Reginald Hart, Lieutenant-Governor of Guernsey.
Guernsey Weekly Press, 1916.

THE DESIRE TO STAND UP
AND BE COUNTED

Although large numbers of local men were fighting for their country, Guernsey did not feature by name in reports from the Front, unlike many other places in the Empire.

Hart was keen for there to be a unit bearing the island's name on the field of battle.

Although it is much closer to the coast of France than to England, Guernsey has had political links with the English Crown since the Norman Conquest of 1066. It had then, as now, an unusual constitutional position in that it is part of the British Isles but not the United Kingdom, and is governed by its own parliament and legislative assembly called the States of Deliberation. Guernsey is "….not a sovereign state but it is not a part of the United Kingdom. Guernsey is part of Her Majesty's possessions, with an independent legislature, and independent judiciary and an executive consisting of committees which are answerable only to the legislature and not to any other body or authority outside the island".[8] As a 'peculiar of the Crown', the island has the right to be self-governing in terms of home affairs without interference from Parliament, but it remains under U.K. protection. One effect of this special relationship with the Crown is that no

Guernseyman can be conscripted to serve overseas except to rescue the Monarch or to help in the recapture of the British mainland. However this special privilege was overturned for the first time ever with the formation of the Royal Guernsey Light Infantry.

Hart persuaded the States of Guernsey to authorise an offer to the War Office of a complete Infantry Service Battalion in order to show the island's devotion to the Crown. On 28th June 1916 the States of Deliberation were asked to deliberate "As to the measure which it may be thought advisable to adopt with a view to placing at His Majesty's disposal, for service overseas during the present war, all men from 18 to 41 years of age who may be available in the islands of the Bailiwick, with the exception of Alderney." Alderney had always organised its Militia in a different way and this may be why they were considered an exception at this stage. Despite this, many men from Alderney were to fight and some would suffer injury or death while serving with the Royal Guernsey Light Infantry. According to local newspapers, after hearing stirring speeches from the Lieutenant Governor, the Bailiff and others the States decided to adopt the principle *with acclamation and rising from their seats the members sang the National Anthem with enthusiasm"*

of compulsory military service. This ended men of the Bailiwick's long exemption from conscription except in very special circumstances.

The reporter on the scene noted that it was agreed by the States "with acclamation and rising from their seats the members sang the National Anthem with enthusiasm". This patriotic enthusiasm did not take into account the experiences of other communities on the mainland where "Pals" Battalions were formed only to be decimated soon after. Many small communities were devastated by heavy losses in a single battle, affecting everyone in the town, village or workplace. Nearly two months later on the 22nd of August 1916 a *Projet-de-Loi* was brought forward for consideration and adopted by the States of Guernsey. The *Projet* was based on the English Military Service Act but with one important difference. On the proposition of the Reverend J. Penfold, who became the Dean of Guernsey soon afterwards, the clause providing for the exemption of conscientious objectors was deleted. This meant that no Guernseyman could escape conscription by reason of conscience. A Guernsey Law has to come before the island's legislature in the form of a *Projet-de-Loi* for

approval by a majority vote. The *Projet* must then have the sanction of the King or Queen in Council and must be registered before the Royal Court before it has the force of law in the island. This particular Order in Council was finally registered on Thursday November 16th 1916 at a special sitting of the Royal Court. Following this, for the first time men of the Bailiwick of Guernsey could be called up for compulsory military service overseas.

THE CONSCRIPTION ACT

The Conscription Act[9] came into force across the Bailiwick 30 days later. On the 17th of December 1916, following the suspension of the Royal Guernsey Militia for the duration of the war, the Royal Guernsey Light Infantry was formed. Its name was chosen by the War Office. Due to the Conscription Act brothers Latimer and Herbert Le Poidevin and hundreds of local men like them had no choice but to go overseas to fight on the Western Front. Officers and men of the Guernsey contingents of the 6th Battalion the Royal Irish Regiment and the 7th Battalion the Royal Irish Fusiliers returned to the island to form the nucleus of the 1st (Service) Battalion of the new Regiment. Eligible men were then called up an age group at a time, the first group consisting of some sixty 19 year olds. This call up continued until the Service Battalion was at full strength. Lists of names of the latest batch to be conscripted appeared in the newspapers every week.

There was the possibility of appeal to a Tribunal on the grounds of work or family commitments, which might result in a delay of a few months if approved. The 2nd (Reserve) Battalion was then formed mainly from new recruits, older men and those less physically fit. They were to form a Home Depot Battalion but also acted as a reserve to provide drafts of replacements as necessary for the Service Battalion. Meanwhile the ladies of the island under the lead of the Bailiff's wife Mrs E.C. Ozanne took on the task of providing colours, bugles and drums for the new Regiment.

The New Year of 1917 began with the two Battalions of the Royal Guernsey Light Infantry undergoing initial training at various sites around the island including L'Ancresse, Les Beaucamps and Fort George.

They then paraded at the Castle Emplacement on the 28th of February after a route march around the island. Together with the 109th Company, Royal Garrison Artillery and 2nd (Home Service) Battalion of the North Staffs Regiment they were inspected by the Lieutenant Governor. Newspaper reports of the day show that the streets of St Peter Port were decorated with flags and bunting for the event, and the parade appears to have taken the form of a triumphal procession through the town. On the 3rd of May 1917 all of the troops raised in the Bailiwick under the Military Service Act paraded together at L'Ancresse.

Presentation of drums, bugles, flags and medals to the 1st (Service) Battalion of the Royal Guernsey Light Infantry on L'Ancresse Common on 3rd May 1917.
GMAG 4785. © Guernsey Museum.

Present were the 109th Company, Royal Garrison Artillery, the 166th Company, Royal Engineers and the 1st (Service) Battalion and 2nd (Reserve) Battalion of the Royal Guernsey Light Infantry. The troops marched to L'Ancresse in the morning, had their lunch on the Common, then the presentation of flags, drums and bugles took place during the afternoon before a huge crowd who had gathered from all over the island. The Bailiff's wife presented the gifts from the island's women to the Battalion, and more "stirring speeches" were given by the Lieutenant Governor, the Bailiff and Major A.H.P. Davey.

On the 1st of June 1917 the 1st Battalion RGLI paraded for inspection at the Fort Field at Fort George before marching to the White Rock in St Peter Port to board the boat that would take them to England for further training before going to the Front. It was the first time that a fighting unit bearing the island's name had gone overseas. This is the background against which the notebook is set. Private Le Poidevin's account of his experiences in the Great War starts when he joined up in January 1917, and ends with his return to the island after demobilisation in 1919.

GUERNSEY
TRAINING

" No. 656
Pte. Le Poidevin. L.T.
C Company
First Service Battalion
Royal Guernsey Light Infantry

Some of my experiences while on
Active Service from the time I joined
up to the time I got demobilised.
First, age of enlistment 24 11/12,
and date when joined up the 9th of
January, 1917, and got demobilised
on the 23rd of June 1919. The
starting of my training was at Fort
George, Guernsey and at Beaucamp,
also on L'Ancresse Common where
we passed our shooting.

top
Sergeant Banneville and Corporals Le Moignan and Collings giving instruction to men
of the RGLI in the use of the Short Magazine Lee Enfield Mk III rifle. Les Beaucamps,
Guernsey. Circa early 1917.

The Barry Jones Collection. © Guernsey Museum.

above
Men of the RGLI practicing laying barbed wire. Fort George Field, Guernsey.
Circa early 1917.

The Barry Jones Collection. © Guernsey Museum.

right
Men in No. 3 Platoon of the 2nd (Reserve)
Battalion, RGLI on a trench digging exercise.
Fort George environs, Guernsey. Circa early 1917.

The Barry Jones Collection. © Guernsey Museum.

right
Sergeants Banneville and Baker overseeing target shooting practice for men of the 2nd
(Reserve) Battalion, RGLI. Grandes Rocques, Guernsey. Circa early 1917.

The Barry Jones Collection. © Guernsey Museum.

GUERNSEY
TRAINING

right
Men in No.3 Platoon of the 1st (Service) Battalion, RGLI undergoing instruction in firing the .303 calibre Lewis Mk 1 Light Machine Gun. Fort George, Guernsey. Circa early 1917.

The Barry Jones Collection. © Guernsey Museum.

far right
Captain Moore giving instruction to the men of the RGLI. Grandes Rocques, Guernsey. Circa early 1917.

The Barry Jones Collection. © Guernsey Museum.

bottom right
The tug-of-war team of 'A' Company, RGLI competing at the Gymkhana on 24th May 1917, Guernsey.

The Barry Jones Collection. © Guernsey Museum.

below
The tents of 'A' Company, RGLI in camp. Grandes Rocques, Guernsey. Circa early 1917.

The Barry Jones Collection. © Guernsey Museum.

OFF TO WAR

1917 1ST JUNE

❝ *After a few months training, the Battalion came under orders for overseas, leaving Guernsey on the 1st of June 1917 for England, but as I was kept back in the rear guard, I did not leave before the 14th of June 1917, taking the Battalion pet Joey with us.*❞

left
Men of the 1st (Service) Battalion, RGLI gathered on the quayside at the White Rock, St. Peter Port Harbour. Waiting to board the steamship that will take them to England. Probably 1st June 1917.
© Guernsey Museum.

right
Officers and men of the RGLI with the regiment's mascot 'Joey' on the quayside on their day of departure. White Rock, St. Peter Port Harbour, Guernsey. 1st June, 1917.
GMAG 4728. © Guernsey Museum.

OFF TO WAR

Private Le Poidevin notes that he enlisted in the 1st (Service) Battalion, Royal Guernsey Light Infantry on the 9th of January 1917. The unit had only been formed towards the end of the previous month so he was one of the earliest conscripts. The information he provides about his training is confirmed by local newspaper reports of the day and also in a booklet entitled *Sarnia's Record in the Great War*,[10] published soon after the war ended. The majority of the Battalion left the island for further training on the 1st of June 1917, following parades and presentations of drums, bugles and colours at L'Ancresse. The Battalion "pet" or mascot was a donkey called Joey.

Guernsey people are traditionally called donkeys because of their supposed stubbornness, and the story goes that before departure the men of the RGLI were invited to choose a mascot. The options were an Irish wolfhound, presumably because many of the

men had been in Irish regiments before, or a donkey. The latter was the almost unanimous choice, and was presented to the battalion by Colonel St Leger Wood D.S.O., A.A., Q.M.G. Joey had previously pulled a milk cart for a farmer Ash of Le Bouet, but he was given a new harness decorated in the island colours of green and white and placed at the head of the parade to the harbour. For various reasons he did not leave with the main contingent, but like Private Le Poidevin went to England with the rear guard two weeks later.

above
Sergeant Pearce, Private Le Page and men of the 1st (Service) Battalion, RGLI on board the steamer bound for Southampton. Circa June 1917.
The Barry Jones Collection. © Guernsey Museum.

above right
Men of the 1st (Service) Battalion RGLI passing through a small hamlet in the Kent countryside on a training route march. Bourne Park Camp environs, near Canterbury. Circa June 1917.
© Guernsey Museum.

Private Le Poidevin goes on to note:

1917 15TH JUNE

> We arrived at Southampton on the 15th, taking the train from Southampton to Waterloo, and from Waterloo station we marched to Victoria station. We left in a train for East station, Canterbury, arriving on the same day, and marched from the station up to Bourne Park camp, just outside a little village called Bridge, where the Battalion was stationed. From this camp we had about three miles to the town of Canterbury, where we passed many a happy hour, and also at Sandwich and Deal which was about 17 miles from Bourne Park.
>
> After being in this camp a few months, they began sending men on leave and my turn came on the 10th of Sep 1917, with the last lot that was sent from the camp.
>
> We got in the train at Canterbury and arrived at Weymouth at midnight, where we took the boat for Guernsey arriving on the 11th September, leaving again on the 15th and arriving at Southampton on the 16th where we took a straight run for Canterbury. Not long before I arrived, we had orders to clear up, as we were on the move for France. Yet before leaving this camp the boys did not forget to help themselves to the canteen, damage done to over £100. Anyhow we made the best of it, then early on the morning of the 25th of September 1917 we marched down to the station and took the train for Southampton, where we embarked for France on the 27th of Sep 1917."

Bourne Park was a large house whose grounds housed training camps for various regiments at this stage of the war. The surrounding area of the Kent countryside and coast was used for map work and route marches. Troops also had instruction in skills such as firing Lewis guns and bomb throwing. There was an emphasis on sports and fitness, with teams from different regiments competing in football, running races and boxing. Some of the men also took part in rifle shooting training and contests at Bisley in Surrey. *The Kentish Gazette* of October 6th 1917 mentions the presence of the RGLI at Bourne Park in an article entitled "Decoration for a Guernsey Man". It goes on to say that, "An interesting presentation was made at the camp of the Guernsey Battalion, near Canterbury, a few days ago, the Military Medal being presented to Sergt. George Alfred Walden by Major-General the Hon C. E. Bingham, commanding the 67th Division. The investiture took place at a parade of the Battalion. Sergt. Walden (then a Lance-Corp.) was awarded the medal for his gallantry while serving with the Royal Irish Regiment."

ON TO
FRANCE

This presentation must have been one of the last events before their pre-embarkation leave, which was in September 1917. Mrs Marie de Garis was a child at the time and in conversation in 2009 she related that the West United Agricultural and Horticultural Show was on when the men came home on leave, and some of them went a bit wild, leaping over the benches and sampling the fruit and other produce. She added that nobody minded because they knew what "the boys" were going back to when they left for France. Local newspapers of the era were filled with lists of casualties of the war and details of various battles on land and at sea, so nobody had any doubt about the dangers. The RGLI paraded through Town before leaving the island to a great send-off from hundreds of islanders gathered at the harbour.

They went back to Bourne Park for a short time before travelling by train to Southampton from where they embarked for France. Their mascot Joey stayed behind in England for a while then eventually returned to his old job of pulling a milk cart in Guernsey.

The Battalion War Diary for the 1st (Service) Battalion, Royal Guernsey Light Infantry starts at this point and covers the period from September 1917 to April 1918. It notes that 44

Officers and 964 Other Ranks travelled in three trainloads to Southampton, arriving between 10.30 and 12.30 on 26th September 1917, each man carrying his own rations. Animals, cycles (which were the responsibility of "D" Company signallers) and vehicles were included in the third trainload, which consisted of grooms, the Commanding Officer, his batman, the Regimental Quarter Master Sergeant, the Transport Officer, the Medical Officer and 70 Other Ranks. These roles are essential to the efficient functioning of the Battalion but they tend to be overlooked when people think about a fighting force. Light Infantry Regiments had bands consisting of buglers and drummers, but the RGLI Bandsmen were to parade with their Companies rather than as a band. From Southampton they all boarded the *Southwestern Miller* which sailed for Le Havre at 18.00, arriving at 06.30 on the 27th. No-one was allowed to leave the train without permission, and the journey across the Channel was to be treated as a night march, with no noise or lights permitted.

The *Southwestern Miller* [11] was used regularly for cross channel journeys between Southampton and Le Havre during the war years. Another soldier who crossed on it in February 1918 describes it as "... an airy craft for a night crossing of the English Channel. The stalls were bare of everything but the hard floors. It was an uncomfortable night. We arrived at Le Havre, France, at four o'clock the next morning, having been convoyed across by a fleet of destroyers. Out thru Spithead past the Isle of Wight, with the city of Portsmouth on our left, we sailed and before entering the Channel waited for our convoy to be made up. Flashlights soaring into the heavens were searching for enemy aircraft all about us. Dozens of these lights played in the air. Just the night before the City of Dover, on the Channel and not far from us had been shelled by

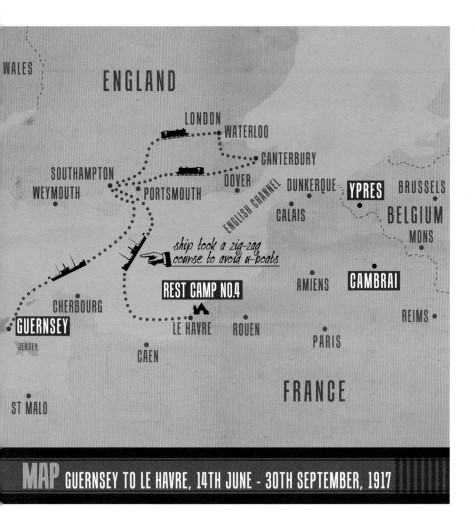

MAP GUERNSEY TO LE HAVRE, 14TH JUNE - 30TH SEPTEMBER, 1917

U-boats, while London had been raided again by air bombers. It was a moonlight night and a bad night to be afloat, but the watch dogs again calmed our fears. The distance from Southampton to La Havre is 106 nautical miles and our zig-zag course probably increased the distance one-quarter." From Le Havre the RGLI marched to a rest camp where they stayed until the 30th of September.

> *the Quarries in which we saw some of the Guernsey boys working."*

Private Le Poidevin notes:

> *We landed at Le Havre, this being about six o'clock in the morning, then we marched to No. 4 Rest camp and stayed there for four days. Then one Sunday afternoon we marched from this camp to a station in Le Havre, and arriving in this station the first I noticed was these cattle trucks and written on them was 40 men or 8 horses. Then the next thing was getting up in these trucks and starting for our journey, this being on the 30th of September. During that night we slept the best way we could, as there were no beds, then when daylight came we had a very nice view of different places as we passed along. One of the places was Etaples, also the Quarries in which we saw some of the Guernsey boys working."*

1917 27TH SEPTEMBER

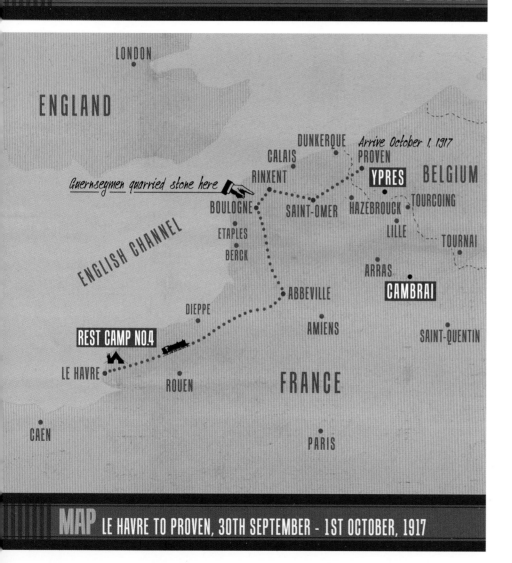

MAP LE HAVRE TO PROVEN, 30TH SEPTEMBER - 1ST OCTOBER, 1917

THE QUARRY COMPANIES

321 Quarrying Company, Royal Engineers was raised in Guernsey and worked in the quarries at Marquise, near Boulogne, from February 1917. It was based at Highcliffe Camp, near Rinxent. Incidentally the railway station there is still called Haut-Banc, a direct translation of High Cliff. The Guernsey quarrymen were mainly employed in quarrying stone for ballast on the railways and for road making. They worked round the clock in 8-hour shifts with a quota to fulfil on each shift. The Company was formed in January 1917 from Guernseymen working in the Bailiwick's granite quarries, who volunteered for overseas service. The men wore Royal Engineers' uniforms and were subject to Army law but received no military training. Their officers were former Guernsey quarry managers. One survivor, interviewed by Parks[12] said: "We expected to be a private company, but when we got out there we found they had sent us a Sergeant Major, Quartermaster Sergeant, pay office and all." Expecting to work as civilian quarrymen, they were surprised to be suddenly treated as soldiers, albeit non-combatant.

> **"**
> *Chums, you're going the wrong way"*

Private Le Poidevin notes:

> **"** *At one station we stopped a while alongside a Red Cross train loaded with wounded from Belgium, so as our train moved on they called out to us, "Chums, you're going the wrong way". My word, I have thought since they were quite right. Then, as night was falling, and knowing we would not arrive before the next morning, it was not very cheerful for us to pass another night like the night before. About midnight on that evening as the train stopped, the order was given to put our packs on, as we were landed and the first thing we noticed as we got out was an air-raid, with anti-aircraft guns and machine guns going off, we began to think this must not be much of a quiet place."*

1917 30TH SEPTEMBER

ONWARDS
BY TRAIN

The Battalion War Diary shows that on the 30th of September, all members of the 1st (Service) Battalion, Royal Guernsey Light Infantry went as a single trainload from their rest camp at Le Havre to Proven (International Corner Station) via Abbeville, Boulogne and St Omer, arriving in Proven at 22.30 on the 1st of October. In 1915, the British Army had built a railway from the Flanders coast to the Western Front. Troops and supplies were carried in one direction, whilst wounded men came in the other direction, mainly from Casualty Clearing Stations placed at intervals along the track. Part of this railway ran from Poperinghe to Westvleteren where there is now a road. International Corner Station where the RGLI men left the train stood behind what is now house no. 58 on that road, near St. Sixtus Abbey.

Private Le Poidevin reported seeing a Red Cross train while they were on their way to the Front. During the First World War the British Red Cross operating with the Order of St John as the Joint War Committee recruited and trained thousands of volunteers who served alongside professional staff mainly in the UK, but also overseas. As well as running hospitals they supplied motorised ambulances to the battlefields, with the first convoy arriving in France in September 1914. Before this ambulances had been mainly horse drawn. As more men were called up to fight, women were also trained to drive these ambulances. Trains and boats were also equipped and staffed by the Red Cross to act as mobile hospitals and it was one of their trains on its way to the coastal ports that the RGLI men encountered.

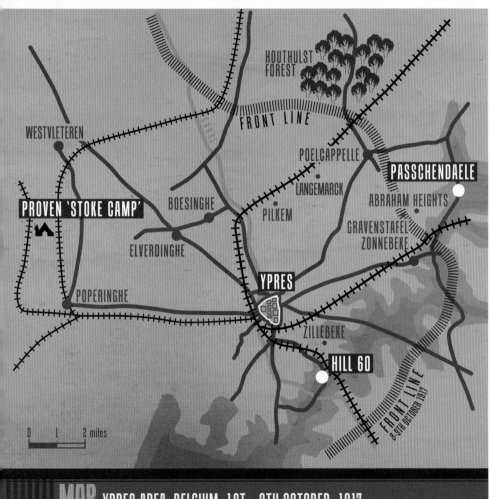

MAP YPRES AREA, BELGIUM, 1ST - 9TH OCTOBER, 1917

Map labels: HOUTHULST FOREST, FRONT LINE, WESTVLETEREN, POELCAPPELLE, PASSCHENDAELE, LANGEMARCK, ABRAHAM HEIGHTS, PROVEN 'STOKE CAMP', BOESINGHE, PILKEM, GRAVENSTAFEL, ZONNEBEKE, ELVERDINGHE, YPRES, POPERINGHE, ZILLEBEKE, HILL 60, FRONT LINE 6-9TH OCTOBER 1917

Scale: 0 — 1 — 2 miles

IN BELGIUM–
UNDER FIRE

Private Le Poidevin and his fellow Guernseymen were now in Belgium, in an area already bearing the scars of earlier battles. He appears to have had some communication problems on arrival, as this was a Flemish speaking area. He notes:

> *This place was in the direction of Ypres in Belgium. Now, after every company had formed up, we started for our new camp. In going along we noticed that most of the buildings had been brought down by shell fire, and had to pick our way as we marched along the roads as they was in an awful state. Then we arrived at our camp which was in a wood, and so many men to every tent also in bivouacs, this being on the 2nd of Oct 1917. The next morning after a little rest and a clean up we had a walk around, many camps to be seen but very little houses, not many civilian people, and the worst with these Belgium people, they did not understand French or English, made it bad for us. This camp was called Stoke camp and the village called Westvleteren, Ypres. After being in this camp a week or so they sent part of the Battalion up the line as stretcher bearers and on working fatigues which was mending roads, all under shell fire."*

1917 2ND OCTOBER

> *This was the first time that the Guernsey battalion was near the firing line; this was up at Langemarke, Ypres and the starting of casualties in the Guernsey Battalion. In arriving at Stoke camp we joined the 29th Division and was put in the 86 Brigade. There was only part of C Company and part of D Company that went up the line, and I was with some of those that stayed in the camp.*
>
> *While the boys was gone we were sent to clean up roads as we had had a lot of rain. We had also dug about 18 inches of earth inside our tents, also filled up sand bags and placed them around our tents to protect us from shrapnel from bombs and the anti-aircraft guns. We were not long after this rain before being flooded out of this camp. One morning we were standing up over our boots with water, holding our stuff in our arms, keeping it from getting wet. It was dangerous to cross this camp night time for holes and mud. Well about two weeks after the boys had left us, they arrived to tell us the news of what they had seen, and I was also pleased to see my brother back with me again, as he was with Major Le Page when he got killed by a shell."*

Pioneers of the 16th Royal Irish Regiment filling in a German trench running across the road to Ribecourt, near Cambrai. 20th November 1917.

Q6288. © Imperial War Museums.

> *mending roads, all under shell fire."*

Prolonged artillery shelling and winter rains reduced parts of the Western Front to a quagmire.

Q42233 (detail). © Imperial War Museums.

SETTING
TO WORK

The RGLI moved into Belgium at a time when the Third Battle of Ypres, sometimes referred to as Passchendaele, was drawing to a close. The historian Correlli Barnett[13] described the area saying that "... the battlefield was a swamp that swallowed men, guns and machines" and he describes the nearby village of Passchendaele as "... no more than a brick coloured smear in the welter of cratered mud".

They arrived at Stoke camp at 3 a.m. on the 2nd of October and remained there until the 9th of October. At this time there was sporadic but fierce fighting in the area. They were attached to the 29th Division, originally a Regular Army division but by this stage of the war many of its original soldiers had been lost and replaced by conscripts and drafts from many different regiments. Initially groups of RGLI men were attached to various regiments with more experience of trench warfare in order to get experience of a wide range of duties.

According to the	14 signallers	ATTACHED 29TH DIVISION SIGNALLING COMPANY ROYAL ENGINEERS
Battalion War Diaries	50 men from C Company	ATTACHED ASSISTANT DIRECTOR, MEDICAL SERVICES, 29TH DIVISION
these attachments were	A Company (strength 189)	ATTACHED 1/2 18TH MONMOUTHS (PIONEERS)
as follows:	D Company (strength 194)	ATTACHED 1/2 18TH MONMOUTHS (PIONEERS)

Pioneer battalions were raised during the war to take over fatigue duties from the infantrymen, freeing them for front line action. These duties included trench digging, installation of barbed wire entanglements, road mending and moving of supplies and munitions. Private Le Poidevin's description of RGLI men road mending, filling sandbags and stretcher bearing matches this information.

Battalion documents show that men on H.Q. duties, buglers and drummers were left behind in camp, and only one officer went forward with each platoon. Private Le Poidevin was in C Company and was one of those who stayed behind in camp. He was not a bugler or drummer so presumably was on H.Q. duties. Those who went forward had to take with them Lewis guns and ammunitions, field cookers and limbers, which were simple two-wheeled carts. A water cart and another limber containing 100 shovels also accompanied them. They travelled by train from Stoke Camp to Pezelhoek then on to their final destination which is not stated. The report notes that the signallers took part in operations in the vicinity of Langemarck Church on the 9th and 10th of October and obtained a good report on their work.

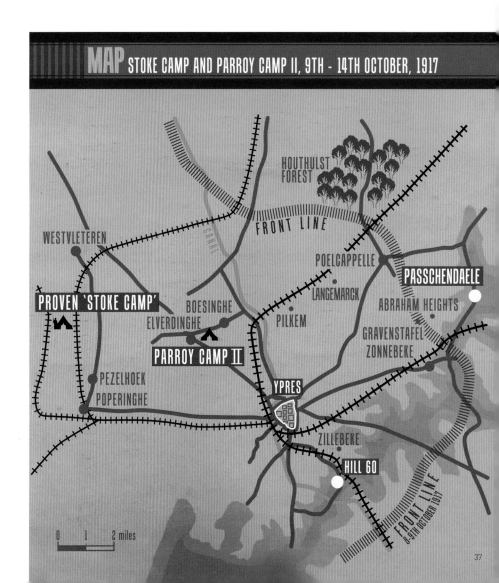

MAP STOKE CAMP AND PARROY CAMP II, 9TH - 14TH OCTOBER, 1917

FIRST R.G.L.I.
CASUALTIES

British stretcher bearers struggling through the deep mud carrying a wounded comrade. Battle of Pil(c)kem Ridge, near Boesinghe. 1st August 1917.

Q 5935. © Imperial War Museums.

The 50 Other Ranks from C Company were employed as stretcher-bearers in the forward battle area from the 4th to 9th of October. A and D companies were attached to the 1st and 2nd Monmouths, who were based at Parroy Camp II, near Elverdinghe. Every day from the 9th to the 14th of October they went out to the Langemarck area and beyond, for work on the roads in the forward area. The tasks assigned to them were made doubly difficult by the conditions in which they had to work. Thick Flanders mud added to the perils of men carrying an injured comrade on a stretcher across broken ground, with the enemy looking to pick them off at any time. Road mending too must have been hard in conditions of heavy rain, flooding and shell damage.

Battalion Casualty Lists for the period from the 10th to the 14th of October show that this work was not without danger. Barely a week after their arrival in Belgium the first RGLI casualties were announced. These included the death of the Second-in-Command of the Guernsey contingent, Major Archibald Davey.

According to the Battalion records he was killed in action on the 14th of October 1917 along with four men from A Company, one of the groups mending roads in the Langemarcke area. However the Commonwealth War Graves records have one of the men, Private John Slimm dying a day later than the others. This might be explained by the fact that casualty records list him initially as missing. All five are buried in Cement House Cemetery near Langemarcke.

Battalion records show that on the 15th of October all of the groups who had been attached to other units rejoined the RGLI at Stoke Camp. Private Le Poidevin says that he was relieved to see that his brother, 223 Lance Corporal Herbert John Le Poidevin had returned safely as he had been with Major Le Page when he was killed by a shell. This appears to be a mistake by Private Le Poidevin and it is probable that his brother had been with Major Davey, mentioned above as he was in A Company, the same company as the five casualties. Major George William Le Page, of D Company, (Guernsey Contingent) 6th Battalion, Royal Irish Regiment was killed in action on the 26th of January 1916 and is buried in Noeux-les-Mines Communal Cemetery near Bethune in Northern France. However there is no record that L/Cpl Le Poidevin had been in the R.I.R. before transferring to the RGLI and he would only have been 17 in January 1916.

Major Archibald Henry Pingston Davey, RGLI.
Guernsey Weekly Press, 1917.

Wartime advertising poster for Smith's Studio cigarettes. Circa 1914.

1917 OCTOBER

> " *So the same morning me and my brother went for the canteen for fags, which was a good ways away, as there was already 4 days he had done without. We were so pleased to see each other that although it was raining we forgot our great coats. While we were billeted in this camp I went one afternoon to see one of the English cemeteries, this being the first one I visited. My word when I saw the poor boys and how they were buried, in every grave there were 20 bodies, there were thousands buried in the cemetery.*"

MAP MILITARY CEMETERIES, 14TH - 17TH OCTOBER, 1917

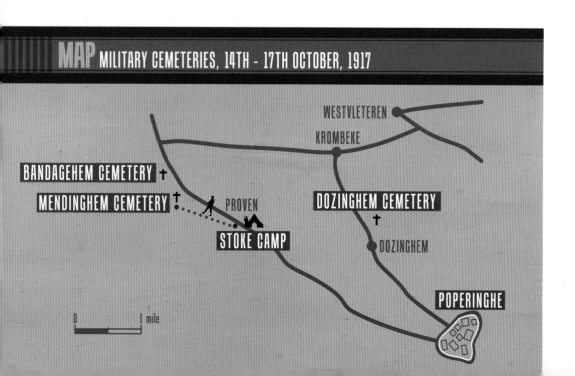

WESTVLETEREN
KROMBEKE
BANDAGEHEM CEMETERY †
MENDINGHEM CEMETERY †
PROVEN
DOZINGHEM CEMETERY †
STOKE CAMP
DOZINGHEM
POPERINGHE

0   1 mile

CAMP LIFE

Cigarettes, known as 'fags', or 'smokes' were part of the basic rations issued to all troops during operations and in camp, so would have been readily available from the canteen. As with rations of alcoholic drinks, they were meant to sustain morale and also helped suppress hunger. At that time the effects of tobacco on health were not well known and as nicotine is addictive, going without cigarettes for four days would have been a real hardship for a regular smoker. Private Le Poidevin then describes his first visit to a war cemetery. Mendinghem Military Cemetery would have been the nearest to his camp as it lies some 500 metres outside the village of Proven. Opened in 1916, it contains 2,391 burials and was part of a group of clearing stations and their associated cemeteries which the troops with typical grim wartime humour named Dozinghem, Mendinghem and Bandagehem.

1917 17TH OCTOBER

Private Le Poidevin notes:
Soon after this the RGLI were on the move again.

"*On the 17th October 1917 we left this camp in the morning, taking the train for France. After arriving at the station, in waiting for our train there, we saw an air-fight which was the first we had seen and saw two aeroplane brought down. Then we started for France, getting out of the train about 2 o'clock in the morning and then started for this new camp. We passed a few villages that had been shelled in the early part of the war, and in going along we could see the places of guns. It made us wonder whether we was going for the firing line or not. Anyhow it was not, so we arrived in this camp about 4 o'clock in the morning on the 18th Oct 1917. This camp was a very fine built place, all the Brigade was camped together and our camp was called No 4 Hendecourt, Arras, France. At this place we got trained with the Brigade for the Battle of Cambrai. This place was in open country, and the Germans had been over this part during the war as there was many German dug-outs which they had made. In the afternoon we used to pull down the wood that lined these dug-outs for our fires night time. We had pleasant time whiles we were billeted at this place. There were sports between the different Regiments that was around there, during the evening there were prayer meetings around our fires at night time.*"

British Bristol Fighter and German Albatross aircraft in aerial dogfight. Watercolour painting by J.S. Merry, 1918.
GMAG 1979.413n. © Guernsey Museum.

DEPOT
TRAINING

Battalion records confirm Private Le Poidevin's recollections, noting that on the 17th of October the Division moved to the VI Corps area near Arras in Northern France and was attached to the Third Army. The RGLI's journey involved marching in three groups from Stoke Camp to Pezelhoek Station, a distance of some 7 km, or just under 5 miles, leaving between 23.00 hours on the 16th of October and 06.00 hours on the 17th. The Battalion went from there by train, a journey of about 100km (just over 60 miles) to Hendecourt to the south east of Arras arriving at 05.00 on the 18th. Here they went into Number 4 Divisional Rest Camp, where they carried out a programme of training in the morning and sports in the afternoon. A draft of 240 men from the 2nd (Reserve) Battalion, RGLI, who had been based back in Guernsey, arrived en route for the Depot training area on the 30th of October, and were accommodated overnight at the camp. On the 2nd of November there was a Brigade ceremonial parade and presentation of medals. Throughout this period in camp the RGLI received training in various tactical schemes. This was particularly rigorous because many of the men were still inexperienced in battle and the planned Cambrai attack would involve the use of many new techniques and skills.

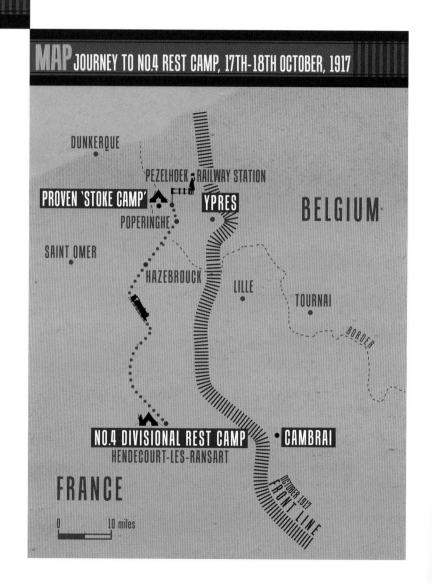

MAP JOURNEY TO NO.4 REST CAMP, 17TH-18TH OCTOBER, 1917

DUNKERQUE

PEZELHOEK RAILWAY STATION

PROVEN 'STOKE CAMP'

YPRES

BELGIUM

POPERINGHE

SAINT OMER

HAZEBROUCK

LILLE

TOURNAI

BORDER

NO.4 DIVISIONAL REST CAMP
HENDECOURT-LES-RANSART

CAMBRAI

FRANCE

OCTOBER 1917 FRONT LINE

0   10 miles

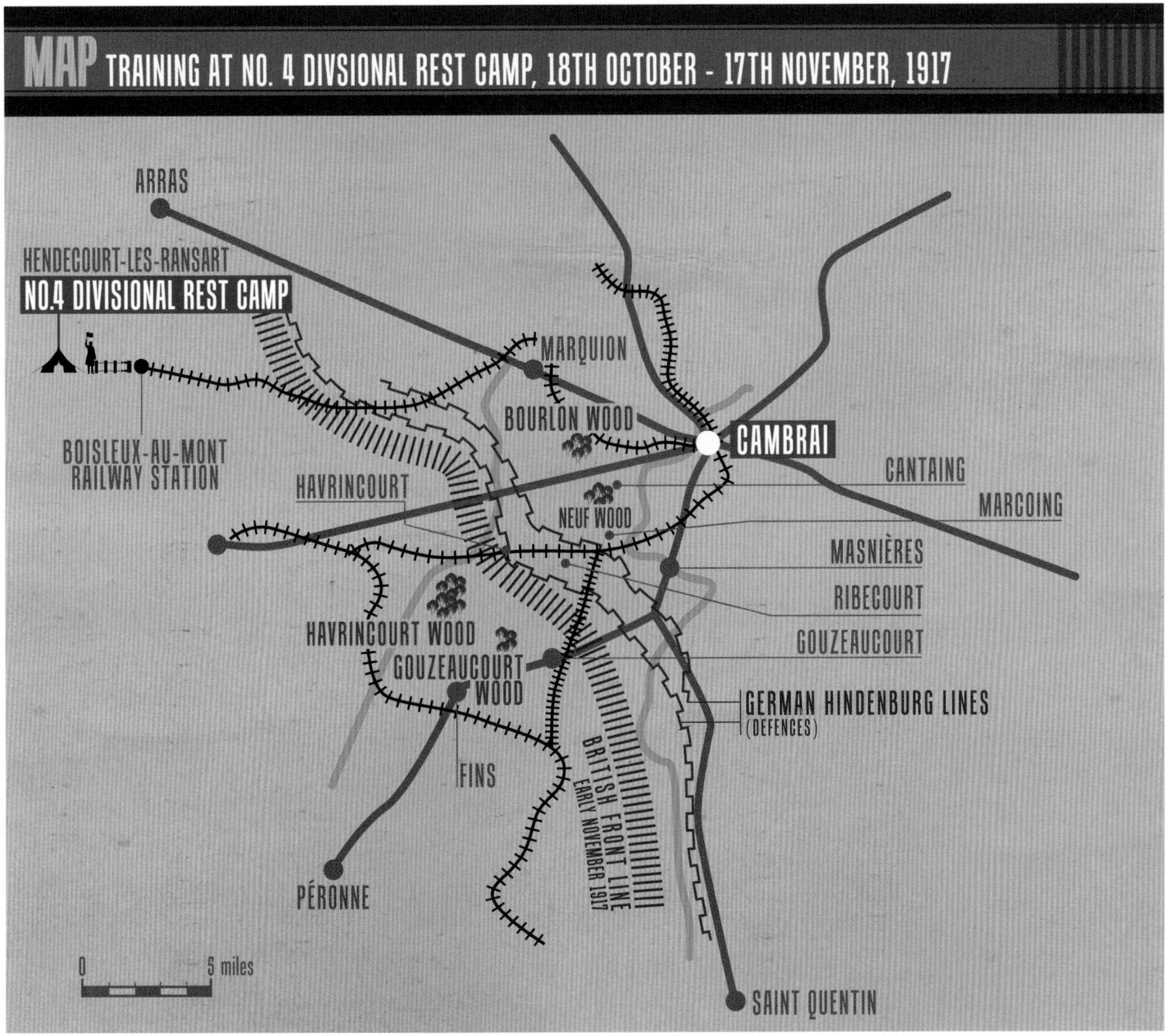

MAP TRAINING AT NO. 4 DIVSIONAL REST CAMP, 18TH OCTOBER - 17TH NOVEMBER, 1917
ARRAS
HENDECOURT-LES-RANSART
NO.4 DIVISIONAL REST CAMP
MARQUION
BOISLEUX-AU-MONT
RAILWAY STATION
BOURLON WOOD
CAMBRAI
CANTAING
HAVRINCOURT
NEUF WOOD
MARCOING
MASNIÈRES
RIBECOURT
GOUZEAUCOURT
HAVRINCOURT WOOD
GOUZEAUCOURT
WOOD
GERMAN HINDENBURG LINES
(DEFENCES)
FINS
BRITISH FRONT LINE
EARLY NOVEMBER 1917
PÉRONNE
0
5 miles
SAINT QUENTIN

> *"the planned Cambrai attack would involve the use of many new techniques and skills."*

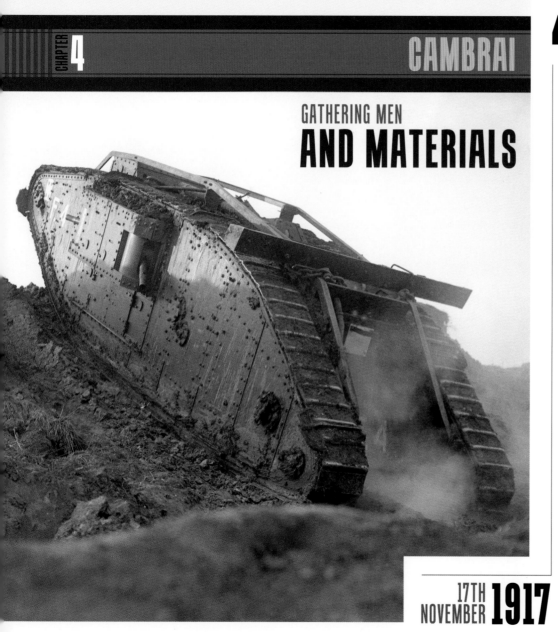

GATHERING MEN
AND MATERIALS

17TH NOVEMBER 1917

> *Then we was quite ready for the Battle which was to start on the following month, we were shown on maps our object which we had to take during this battle, and also had orders given that no prisoners had to be taken unless they were wearing a box-respirator or could give some or any information of how the enemy was situated. Then the order came that the division was moving and that our Brigade would move on the 17th of November. So on the 17th of November in the morning, I was one of those that was chosen for a guard to be sent down to the station to guard the rations for our Battalion. So about 9 o'clock this morning we left this camp Hendecourt for a station called Boisleux-au-Mont. During this day there were different Regiments going away every hour of the day, and our Battalion arrived close on midnight. Then as soon as the rations was loaded up, the train started and we got out of this train near the town of Péronne early on the 18th of Nov 1917. We marched through this town and stayed in a camp just outside of this town, till night time, and as soon as the night was on us, we marched for Fins, which was a very long and weary march. All this work night time was to hide the movements of troops from the enemy. In this village of Fins we got fitted up for a two days battle with ammunition and rations and on the 21st of Nov. 1917, at 2 o'clock in the morning we started for the line well loaded and a distance to walk, many giving up on the way, and not only the walk but we knew it was for a battle and knew that everyone was not coming back."*

> **"**
> *....we knew it was for a battle and knew that everyone was not coming back."*

Official records show that on the 17th of November 1917 the order came through for 86 Brigade to march overnight to Hendecourt, where they would get the train towards the Front. Names of stations are crossed out in the Battalion war diary and replaced with "detraining station". However this first one is referred to as Boisleux later in the document, confirming Private Le Poidevin's recollections. Records also show that eight men and one N.C.O. were detailed to unload the train and guard the blankets and rations which were to be stacked on the platform. Private Le Poidevin would have been included in this group. It was an important task as any rations stolen or lost could not be replaced once they moved up to the Front. Guides from the 3rd Corps of Cyclists were detailed to lead the infantry from the station to their billets. The Army Cyclist Corps was formed in 1914 absorbing a number of pre-existing volunteer cyclist battalions, from the Territorial Force. They were employed mainly as scouts and couriers, but also cycled the canal banks on defensive duties. In difficult terrain such as the thick mud and broken roads of Flanders they often had to abandon their cycles, and because of this the British Army found no long-term role for cyclists so the Corps was disbanded in 1919.

Battalion records show that after leaving camp near Péronne the RGLI marched to Equancourt via Haute Allaire, a distance of more than 10 miles (16 km). They like all the other troops always moved by night so that the Germans wouldn't realise where they were gathering. Equancourt is a tiny village about a mile (1.6km) from Fins, which is where Private Le Poidevin states that they were billeted while they prepared for the Battle of Cambrai. The town of Cambrai had been occupied by the Germans since the autumn of 1914. It was strategically important because it was a significant railhead with links directly back to Germany and was therefore a major point of supply for all the German forces in the northern part of France.

left
Mk IV (female) tank No. F4. Undergoing testing at the Tank Driving School at Wailly, France, in preparation for the Battle of Cambrai. Circa October 1917.
Q 6299. © Imperial War Museums.

PLANNING THE
BATTLE

The German Hindenburg Line near Bullecourt, West of Cambrai.

Q 27520. © Imperial War Museums.

The Canal du Nord passed to the west of the town whilst some 5 miles (8 Km) to the east ran the Canal de L'Escaut (otherwise known as the St Quentin Canal). Late in 1916 the Germans had begun to construct a lengthy and formidable defensive line, known to the British as the Hindenburg line which ran south east from near Lens to Verdun. It incorporated the Canal du Nord and Havrincourt before passing to the north of Trescault where it climbed the Couillet and Bonavis ridges until it met the St Quentin Canal, which it followed southwards for many miles. The section between the two canals was the strongest part. It was up to five miles deep with many rows of heavy gauge barbed wire, deep trenches, pillboxes and dugouts.

It was here that the RGLI was sent as part of the 29th Division.

THE YUKON PACK was a special backpack for carrying equipment. It had a light wood frame which was slightly curved to match the shape of the soldier's back. This frame was inside a canvas sleeve which was held in tension. With the shoulder straps correctly adjusted packs could be carried in a comfortable fashion, high on the back, making carrying even heavy loads over long distances much less exhausting.

Operation Order 8 states that the RGLI marched to the Brigade Assembly Area where they took up position for the attack at 6.20 a.m. It states that:

The original concept for the battle of Cambrai had been a tank raid with limited objectives, but it quickly grew into a full-scale offensive operation. The plan devised by General Byng and his Third Army staff was to use seven Divisions of Infantry and three Brigades of tanks on a 10,000 yard (about 9km) front between the two waterways to break through the Hindenburg Line towards Cambrai.

There would be no lengthy preliminary artillery barrage as had been the custom on the western front, and instead the guns were registered 'silently' on the enemy positions before opening up suddenly as the attack began.

The first assault would be spearheaded by tanks, followed by the infantry who would secure the breach for the cavalry. Private Le Poidevin states that they started for the line on the 21st of November at two in the morning. However official records show that they left Equancourt at 2 a.m. a day earlier, on the night of the 19th/20th of November. The degree of accuracy with which he describes events is probably more surprising than the occasional discrepancy with dates and numbers, given the confusion of battle and the fact that the account was said to have been written when he returned home after demobilisation.

1. The Battalion will move on the night of the 19th/20th to Assembly Area.
2. The Battalion will parade each Company in its own lines at 1.50 a.m.

Order of March:
  D Company
  B Company
  C Company *(Private Le Poidevin's Company)*
  H.Q. (advanced).
  A Company *(His brother, L/Cpl Herbert Le Poidevin's company)*
  Machine Gun Section
  Trench Mortars, Yukon Pack Train
  Intervals of 100 yds (just over 90 m) will be kept between Companies.
  Time   2.24 a.m.
Route EQUANCOURT - FINS cross-roads, thence by track to QUEENS CROSS Rd. junction Q.23 thence into Assembly Area.
Special Attention is to be paid to the following points
1. Absolute silence & no lights.
2. No Smoking.
3. Strict punctuality.

(Note: Author's comments in brackets.)

INTO BATTLE

20TH NOVEMBER 1917

Having already marched some distance, starting at 2.a.m., the men of the RGLI had to prepare themselves for their first experience of a major battle.

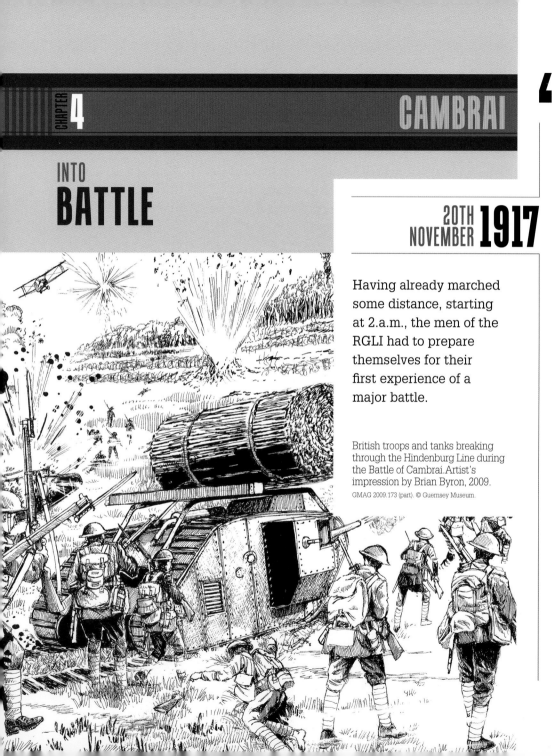

British troops and tanks breaking through the Hindenburg Line during the Battle of Cambrai. Artist's impression by Brian Byron, 2009.
GMAG 2009.173 (part). © Guernsey Museum.

" When at last we reached the front line we were ready for action, only waiting for the guns to start and the order to advance. Then a minute or two before the guns started, our Officer came up and warned us not to get the wind up[14] when the guns would go off, as there was some 800 guns, and over 400 tanks was going over the top before us. Then an hour before day break the barrage started. My word, it was just like a mass of fire lifting from the earth and the working of those tanks coming out from their hiding places.

Then it was our turn to go over the top but we stopped between the old front line of ours and enemy rear we had a little fead[15] but all the same we had our eyes well open. The enemy had started sending shells over which made us keep our heads down as this was new to us. I thought while lying down "It's all very well but what's it when we shall meet the enemy?" There were already dead lying about, then the order came to advance which we did. While we were marching over ground which had been ploughed up by shells I noticed a German aeroplane making its way towards us, and dropping a bomb near us made us quiver. Now the thing was, after advancing all this time, passing over German trenches and along pits that were getting made for placing guns, even the tools was left, and there were groups of Germans passing us just captured, and what surprised me was to see some of our tanks on fire. As our Company, C, was now front line with two tanks working with us, and A company in support we began to attack our object which was Number Nine wood and casualties was small up to this time."

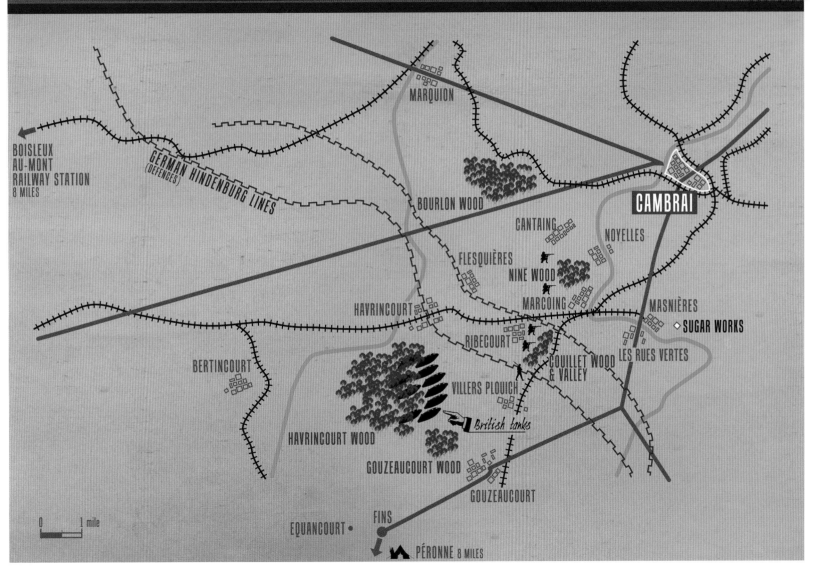

BOISLEUX
AU-MONT
RAILWAY STATION
8 MILES

MARQUION

GERMAN HINDENBURG LINES
(DEFENCES)

BOURLON WOOD

CANTAING

NOYELLES

CAMBRAI

FLESQUIÈRES

NINE WOOD

MARCOING

MASNIÈRES

SUGAR WORKS

HAVRINCOURT

RIBECOURT

COUILLET WOOD
& VALLEY

LES RUES VERTES

BERTINCOURT

VILLERS PLOUICH

British tanks

HAVRINCOURT WOOD

GOUZEAUCOURT WOOD

GOUZEAUCOURT

0   1 mile

EQUANCOURT •   FINS

PÉRONNE 8 MILES

CAMBRAI

" Then it was our turn to go over the top"

British Mk IV (male) tank C23 breaching a German trench during the Battle of Cambrai. Artist's impression by Brian Byron, 2009. GMAG 2009.173 (part). © Guernsey Museum.

Official records show that the battle started exactly as Private Le Poidevin described, with a surprise massed tank attack by the British between the Scarpe and St Quentin. Thirty-six train-loads of tanks had been carried to the assembly positions by the 18th of November, two days before the battle. These tanks were mainly hidden in Havrincourt Wood and where they couldn't be hidden they were camouflaged with canvas painted to represent bricks and tiles so that they would look like buildings. The tanks were supported by the Royal Flying Corps who dropped bombs on gun positions and German strong points to clear a path for the Allied advance. Nineteen divisions of the Third Army were involved in the initial attack. The RGLI formed part of the 29th Division, and were part of the second wave behind the 6th, 12th and 20th Divisions. The first wave had to capture a section of the Hindenburg Line and its support trenches, while the 29th Division was to pass through them and capture the line of the Escaut River, the Canal de St Quentin and the trenches beyond that.

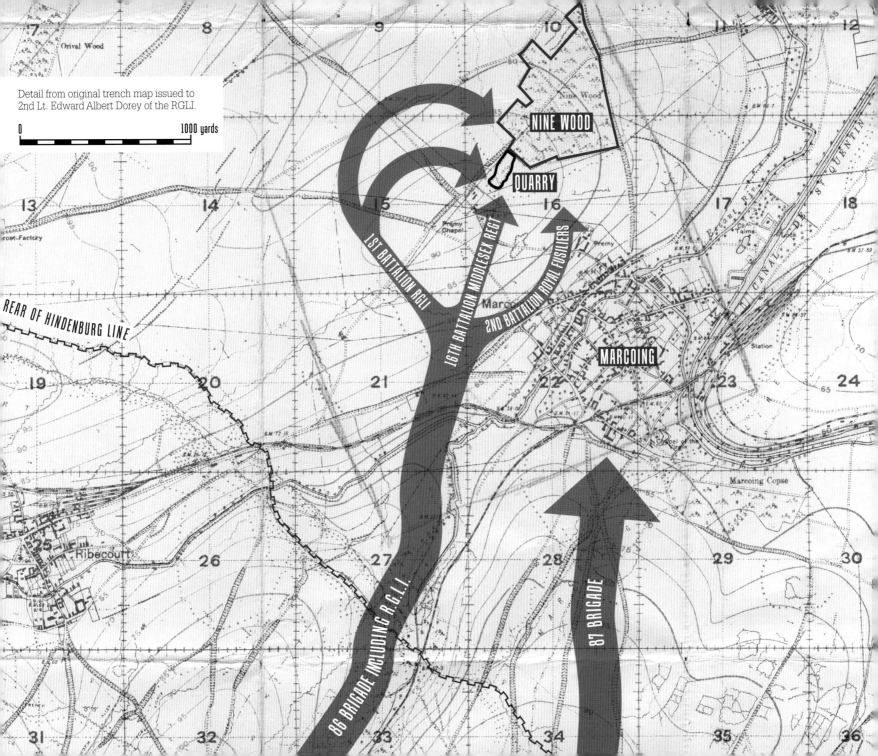

Detail from original trench map issued to
2nd Lt. Edward Albert Dorey of the RGLI.

0   1000 yards

NINE WOOD

QUARRY

1ST BATTALION RGLI

16TH BATTALION MIDDLESEX REGT

2ND BATTALION ROYAL FUSILIERS

REAR OF HINDENBURG LINE

MARCOING

86 BRIGADE INCLUDING R.G.L.I.

87 BRIGADE

Orival Wood

Ribecourt

THE
FIRST DAY

....old Gerry with their machine guns and they opened fire on us."

The way in which British tanks were used in battle at Cambrai was new to the Germans. Their Army Chief of Staff Von Hindenburg stated in his diaries[16] that "... the fact that the tanks had now been raised to such a pitch of technical perfection that they could cross our undamaged trenches and obstacles did not fail to have a marked effect on our troops. The physical effects of fire from machine-guns and light ordnance with which the steel Colossus was provided were far less destructive than the moral effect of its comparative invulnerability. The infantryman felt that he could do practically nothing against its armoured sides. As soon as the machine broke through our trench-lines, the defender felt himself threatened in the rear and left his post."

However Private Le Poidevin's remark about seeing a tank on fire reflects the fact that they were vulnerable to artillery shells. A direct hit could disable or destroy a tank and the fuel would then often catch fire, incinerating its crew. Of the original 476 tanks available on the first day, 65 were lost to German fire, another 71 broke down and 43 got stuck in ditches, trenches and other obstacles.[17] However 8,000 German prisoners were taken in the initial attack and an advance of three to four miles was achieved on a six mile front.

86 Brigade, of which the RGLI was a part, had been given the objective of capturing the Bois des Neufs, or Nine Wood. Its position overlooking the village of Marcoing made its capture essential if the attack was to succeed. So the Brigade advanced up the Couillet valley towards the wood with the Middlesex Regiment in the lead and the RGLI on the left flank. When the Middlesex regiment were held up by an attack at a quarry on the edge of the wood, the RGLI went around them to capture both the quarry and the wood. Private Le Poidevin states that RGLI casualty numbers were relatively small and the official Casualty list shows that five men were killed in action on that first day (one was originally listed as missing). Another twenty seven were wounded, two so seriously that they died a few days later. The Battalion diary reports that the RGLI attacked and "gained the objective (Nine Wood) by 14.00 on the 20th of November, then consolidated their position."

Private Le Poidevin's account of the battle continues with him noting that:

1917 20TH NOVEMBER

> "Being about 4 o'clock, we started to dig ourselves in in front of this wood, and being tired of our tramping and German snipers sniping at us made it a hot place for us, but as night came we had a better chance, and having the news that we were getting relieved by some other regiment the same evening cheered us up. During the night there was a drizzling rain falling that made it bad for us. Early next morning, we had a small counter-attack and A Company came up and helped us to hold our trench. We could see some people coming towards us with long coats and it seemed as if it was women carrying their babies in their arms, but instead it was old Gerry [18] with their machine guns and they opened fire on us.

German 4-man machine gun crew firing their MG 08 from natural cover. Circa 1914-1918.

PUSHING-ON

20TH NOVEMBER **1917**

Wounded British soldiers receiving treatment at a Regimental Aid Post. Artist's impression by Brian Byron, 2009.

GMAG 2009.170 (part). © Guernsey Museum.

> In the evening of the first day as I was busy digging myself in and thinking the quicker I am in shelter the better, someone called out "Here is your brother coming along!", so as he passed my way I looked up and asked him what was he doing around this part, as he belonged to A Company. So he answered that he was attaché to A Company headquarters. During the following day we started to have a few shells over us, and in the afternoon about 4 o'clock this being on the 23rd November got relieved by some other regiment. At the time we got relieved it was a pretty hot place, as shells was dropping nearby every perch.[19] I remember lying down two or three times before getting in the main road. Then we marched to a village called Marcoing which had not been damaged. Our Company got billeted on a French farm. I was with 20 that was in one of these big barns, wet to the skin and full of mud and no clothes to change. So we made the best of it, and after having a good sleep then a brush up, began cleaning our clothes. We were in this place for a 48 hours rest, although we could hear the noise of shells coming from Jerry, and exploding in the village, wondering if they would hit this place. Then the next morning my brother visited me. Of course we had plenty to say after what we had seen, and he said that when he was walking along our trench which was front line that he did not know it at the time.
>
> As it happens I had plenty of what my brother was after and that was cigarettes, so there we were alike. So as dinner time was near and we had to cook our own food, we wished each other good

"

One shell pitched right in our trench, killing six of the boys and wounded many."

luck. But there was no length of time after our parting when a shell hit the barn, hitting upon the beam which was rested upon the wall and I was sitting just in under it. But with a little luck I was not hurt with the crashing of the wall coming down. The boys rushing for the doorway made me cramp up in the corner. As for dust, we could not see each other, and thought that someone was in under the fall, but as the dust cleared I looked around. There was only the rifles and equipment buried and two of the boys hit, and as things was cleared, I ran in the open fields as Gerry's planes was over. I stayed in the open till night time thinking no more of our food. Well the same evening, which was the 25th, we got ready for the firing line again, marching for the Cambrai front, and relieved a regiment at six o'clock the same evening. After taking over these trenches we began doing them up, as only at night there was a chance of working. The next night the enemy gave us a rosy time, I thought every minute that we was going to get buried in

our trenches, we could hear nothing else but the whistling of bullets and shells. One shell pitched right in our trench, killing six of the boys and wounded many.[20]

Then, as things came quiet, they asked for men to carry the dead and wounded down by a canal, so I was helping the first lot. There was a small hill to climb which was very dangerous. We spent 5 days in these trenches. One of the last days it was very sunny, and when I was sitting in the trench I could see a village in a valley a ways off, and during the time I was sitting there, three German aeroplanes came over and made the round of this village. But no sooner were they back to their line than their field guns began shelling this village, it wasn't long before the village being to the ground.

Well as for many night time in these trenches it was bitter cold and the only way of getting warm was working, we was longing to get right out of it. On the evening of the 28th Nov at 6 o'clock we got relieved and marched down into a village called Masnières for a rest in the cellars."

The Battalion diary confirms Private Le Poidevin's report of "...old Gerry with their machine guns", noting that at 08.00 on the 21st of November an enemy counter-attack from the North was driven off. Twelve men were injured in this incident. Official records confirm that the Battalion was relieved at 5 p.m. and then marched to Marcoing where they went into billets. They stayed there for two days, then at 16.30 on the 23rd of November they left Marcoing and took over the line at Masnières.

STALEMATE

MASNIÈRES AND LES RUES VERTES

The overall situation settled into a familiar stalemate in the week following the Allied successes of the 20th of November. The canal had been captured, and some bridgeheads had been established on the far side. RGLI casualty numbers had been relatively low, with eight men being killed in action and about forty suffering wounds. Rather than fighting a full scale battle, the role of the 29th Division reverted to holding the section of the line between Marcoing and Masnières. There were frequent trench raids and sporadic shelling from both sides so casualties continued to occur among the ranks of the RGLI. Sadly one of these was Private Le Poidevin's younger brother Lance Corporal Herbert John Le Poidevin.

On the 27th of November Lieutenant Colonel Hart-Synnot, D.S.O., who was the nephew of Guernsey's Lieutenant Governor Sir Reginald Hart, took over temporary command of the Battalion from Lieutenant Colonel de la Condamine who had sustained an ankle injury. On the 28th of November the Battalion, which was in the 86th Brigade reserve at the time, moved into the catacombs at Masnières and remained there until the morning of the 30th of November. The catacombs or cellars where they waited were part of a huge complex located directly under the Cambrai - St Quentin Road where the D15 crosses over it in the directions of Crèvecoeur and Marcoing. Meanwhile unknown to the Guernsey soldiers the German Army had been using the lull after the first attack to organise a full scale counter-attack involving 20 Divisions. The counter-attack was to last until the 3rd of December, during which period the British held most of the area that they had gained ten days earlier but lost an area almost as large to the south of it. In doing so they suffered many casualties, including a large number of RGLI men. Private Le Poidevin recorded his experiences of this period.

" so he says "Yes, he got killed three days ago"

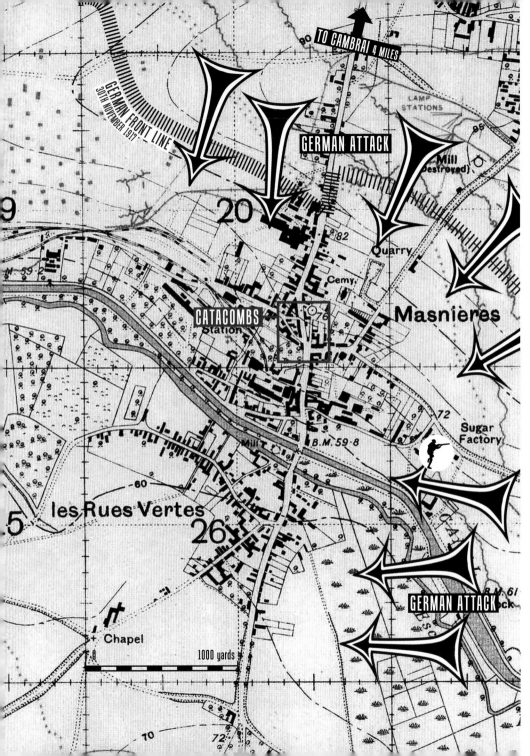

Original British WW1 trench map showing the town of
Masnières and its southern suburb, Les Rues Vertes (detail).
Note: German trenches and other enemy defences are
marked in red, corrected to 20th September 1917.

1917 29TH-30TH NOVEMBER

❝ *We were supposed to wait, as a Division
was supposed to relieve ours the next day.
Here we had a jolly good sleep and giving out
mail cheered us up, and there was news of the
different ones that had been killed or wounded.
As I was sitting down reading a letter from home
I heard the next chap to me tell another chap if he
knew that my brother had been killed. So I looked
up and asked if he meant my brother, so he says
"Yes, he got killed three days ago". So what I
done I went and found A Company and saw his
section commander, so I was told of how he met
his death. It was my last thought that a few days
ago when I was giving the cigarettes and we
were wishing each other good luck that it was
the last time seeing each other. It was our parting,
poor boy.*[21] *Then the next morning I thought of
finding the Officer which had his few things, this
being on the 30th of November 1917."*

COUNTER ATTACK
MASNIÈRES AND LES RUES VERTES

1917 30TH NOVEMBER

Latimer's Lewis machine gun team crossing the bridge under German fire, 30th November 1917. Artist's impression by Brian Byron, 2009.
GMAG 2009.174 (part). © Guernsey Museum.

" *But the first thing we heard that morning was an order to stand to as the Germans were attacking the village. There was no time for breakfast; the only chance was to get ready in fighting order. Then we had the orders to move one at the time out of this cellar, and to make our way down the street and line up along the canal banks in trenches that had been made before. So as things was very quiet below we thought it must be about the same on top, but to my surprise when my turn came this street, all I could see and hear was shells hitting both sides of the street and men laying about. My word, I thought, here's something to go through. So with luck I reached the trench safe, now that the morning was almost past and still shells coming over as they were trying hard for the bridges that was built across this canal.*

Close on mid-day an order came from Captain Stranger [22] *that a Lewis Gun team was wanted on his left flank. So as our section was a Lewis gun team we was sent and as it was so dangerous as we had to go over one of these bridges, our Officer said that only two was to go at a time, and the last two was to carry a box of ammunition. So I was one of them that stopped to carry it. Now the thing was, not to lose sight of the others or we were going*

to be lost altogether. It wasn't much of a place for any man to be in the open as there was a little too much shrapnel flying about. Then we started with this box, carrying our rifles on our shoulders and while crossing the bridge the other chap lost his strength which left me alone with this box and I suppose with a little fright as shells was dropping too near to please me. So I managed the best way I could, I reached the other end in a short time, but by the time I reached there I had lost sight of the others.

On this side of the canal the ground was low and wet and very tall grass growing so I crawled through till I found the others with the box. We stayed in this muddy place till night before being able to stand up or walk about. Nearly every minute during that afternoon we thought it was our last, but now that night time was upon us we had a chance to walk about and keep ourselves warm, and about midnight when an Officer visited us we reminded him that we hadn't seen food yet that day."

"only the top of the building was blown in and the bottom was a cellar"

Horsfall and Cave's[23] description of the battle of the 30th of November confirms Private Le Poidevin's recollections. They note that "... At 7a.m. the German attack started with heavy artillery and machine gun fire on the Brigade's position. By 9 a.m. the German attack began with a movement of infantry out of the Masnières – Beaurevoir line under the protective machine-gun fire of low flying aircraft. ... at 10.30 am the Germans attacked 86 Brigade, which was in part of the outer edge of the Masnières – Beaurevoir line at Noyelles.... Lines of men were seen....advancing from behind their line out of Crèvecoeur and towards Mon Plaisir Farm. Despite heavy fire from the British Infantry and a barrage from the Field Artillery, the Germans pressed on towards the North West." The 29th Division's right flank came under attack as the Germans swept through the line by Crèvecoeur. 86 Brigade was ordered to redeploy to meet the threat and the RGLI was sent south of the river and canal to cover the area of Les Rues Vertes, a suburb of Masnières. They held the village but had to retake it twice in what Parks describes as "...heavy and vicious hand-to-hand fighting." However casualties were still relatively light, with six RGLI men being killed in action on the 30th of November and a further 50 or so being wounded or taken prisoner of war. Private Le Poidevin's account continues:

The RGLI fighting hand-to-hand with the Germans amongst the ruins of Les Rues Vertes, 30th November 1917. Artist's impression by Brian Byron, 2009.
GMAG 2009. 174 (part). © Guernsey Museum.

1917 1ST DECEMBER

There was no attacking by the enemy during the night and about 6 o'clock the next morning (1st of December) our Officer came and moved us and took us back over this canal and placed us in front of a sugar factory, only the top of the building was blown in and the bottom was a cellar.

COUNTER ATTACK
MASNIÈRES AND LES RUES VERTES

1917 1ST DECEMBER

> *There was a hole made from outside facing this canal, so we made a small trench between the canal and factory so that during the day when thing was quiet that two men with the gun could stay while the rest could have a sleep in turns in the factory. When came my turn for a sleep it was a case of looking for something to eat, but it was a helpless job. Now the officer has told us that in case of a barrage coming over that everyone was to take shelter in the cellar. As it happen it was my turn in this small trench on duty when this barrage started, so the chap said "It's started! Be off!" so we ran for our life and I being the first with the gun I placed it in the opening of this cellar, so as to have a chance to fire along the canal bank.*

> *So from this hole to get in the cellar was a tunnel of about 6 yards (about 5.5 m) long, so by being first I had to get right through to give the other chap a chance for shelter. But before I was the end of the tunnel a shell hit the other end which caused a lot of wind in the tunnel blowing me right out in the open again.*

> *There I stopped til someone picked me up and took me in. As I had been properly shocked, I remember nothing of being picked up, but soon came around when*

Latimer caught in the factory tunnel explosion,
1st December 1917. Artist's impression by Brian Byron, 2009.
GMAG 2009. 174 (part). © Guernsey Museum.

"
I made very poor blood as it was an unpleasant job, as our gun was out of action..."

in the cellar. As the barrage lifted we started to go back in this trench, and we could see some thousands of Germans advancing, as this place was on a small slope, only the enemy wasn't making their way towards us. We knew something was going to happen, and sure enough they attacked the bridge that led into the main street of the village. Very hard fighting took place, and our battalion being at the bridge head suffered very much in casualties.

Our Officer which was Captain Stranger had collected men of different regiments which held this part of the canal, and about midnight on the 1st of Dec 1917 we were told that the Division was getting relieved. This evening it was lovely moon light, and very quiet, so we marched toward battalion headquarters. As we passed by the bridge three of our gun team was put to watch the bridge, me being one of the three to watch this bridge, being as a rearguard for the battalion to move off. I made very poor blood as it was an unpleasant job, as our gun was out of action, so while two men was trying to put it together that left me to watch with my rifle, and not a soul was to be heard."

Latimer's machine gun team trying to fix the broken Lewis gun during their night-time rearguard duty, 1st December 1917. Artist's impression by Brian Byron, 2009.

GMAG 2009. 174 (part). © Guernsey Museum.

THE LEWIS GUN

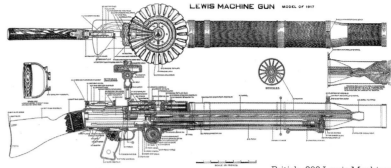

British .303 Lewis Machine Gun image and schematic, 1917.

Private Le Poidevin mentions here that he was a Lewis Gunner. The Lewis Gun was the first truly effective Light Machine Gun used by the British Army. It weighed about 28 lb. (12.7 kg), only about half as much as the typical machine gun of the era, but still quite heavy. It was chosen because it was relatively cheap, and theoretically it could be carried and used by a single soldier, and so move with the troops during advances and retreats. A strong man could even fire it from the shoulder like a rifle while standing, and it was often fired from the hip when moving forwards. It had a circular 47 round drum magazine of ammunition mounted on top, and the loaded spare drums were carried in special webbing carriers. Each man in the machine gun team carried two drums. In addition spares were carried in a wooden box of six which would be very heavy and cumbersome. These would normally be carried by two men except in extreme circumstances such as those described previously by Private Le Poidevin. Carrying a box of 6 drums single handed across a bridge while under enemy fire was no mean feat. The Lewis Gun was a very effective weapon which continued in use until the end of the Second World.

The Battalion War Diary for the 1st of December 1917 states simply that at 07.00 the battalion held defensive positions around Les Rues Vertes and along the canal bank. There was an enemy barrage followed by a strong infantry attack against the Battalion Front. The attack was successfully repulsed, all positions remaining intact. At 3 p.m. there was another enemy barrage and infantry attack forcing the front line to withdraw slightly from Les Rues Vertes. The Battalion then held the line of the canal until they successfully withdrew from Masnières, arriving at the Brown Line at 4 a.m. on the 2nd of December. However the *Guernsey Star* of December 17th 1917 carried on its front page an article from the *Manchester Guardian* of the 10th of December, giving more details of the role of the RGLI at Les Rues Vertes. It describes amongst other things

"
I am told that at least 500 of the enemy were killed by bullets or drowned"

British Lewis machine gunners firing from a winter trench. Circa 1914-1918.

Q 10609. © Imperial War Museums.

the actions of the machine gun crew in the sugar factory, stating that "...We had a number of machine guns in the sugar factory...These machine gunners under a Captain were the bulwark which largely supported the village... A German column which must have been nearly a regiment in strength was sent from Crevecoeur to cross the canal and attack Les Rues Vertes. It was a splendid mark for the machine gunners firing from the sugar factory across the flats and I am told that at least 500 of the enemy were killed by bullets or drowned after falling wounded into the canal as they tried to cross it by a narrow bridge". This matches very closely with Private Le Poidevin's account of events. The captain mentioned here would have been Captain H.E.K. Stranger, who was awarded the Military Cross for his bravery. Also Private Le Poidevin himself was one of the machine gunners mentioned here.

COUNTER ATTACK
MASNIÈRES AND LES RUES VERTES

"

*not having had any
food for two days"*

1917 2ND DECEMBER

Private Le Poidevin
continues with
his recollections,
noting:

*" About 2 o'clock in the morning of the 2nd of Dec 1917, our Officer came back and ordered
us to pack up, and follow him as we was leaving the village altogether. My word we
walked with a light foot, although not having had any food for two days and close on two
weeks that we hadn't shaved or had a good wash. After leaving this bridge we wasn't long
before catching up to our battalion. I remember passing Marcoing village and we stayed in a
trench just outside Marcoing, a trench which the Germans occupied before the battle. When
daylight arrived we had our rations given for the day, so we made the best of them for our
breakfast.*

right
Wounded British soldiers
being tended in a trench
after an assault.

Q 739. © Imperial War Museums.

far right
Detail of an original British
WW1 trench map. Showing
the area to the West of
Masnières and Les Rues
Vertes. The map was issued
to 2nd Lieutenant Edward
Albert Dorey of the 1st
(Service) Battalion RGLI.
Note: German trenches and
other enemy defences are
marked in red, corrected to
20th September 1917.

GMAG 5308.1

*The same morning, after the roll call,
the Battalion was left with 501 men.
Before the battle the Battalion was over
1000 men and 300 men joined us at
Masnières, which made it about 700 men
and N.C.O. casualties, and 18 Officers.[24]
There was also many from different
Regiments that was with us, as they had
lost the trail of their regiment. The same
evening we left Masnières we brought
wounded on stretchers from the factory.
This day in this trench a few of our boys
got wounded, then after spending the
day, a bitter cold day, we move further
back to another village called Ribecourt."*

TO HAVRINCOURT WOOD

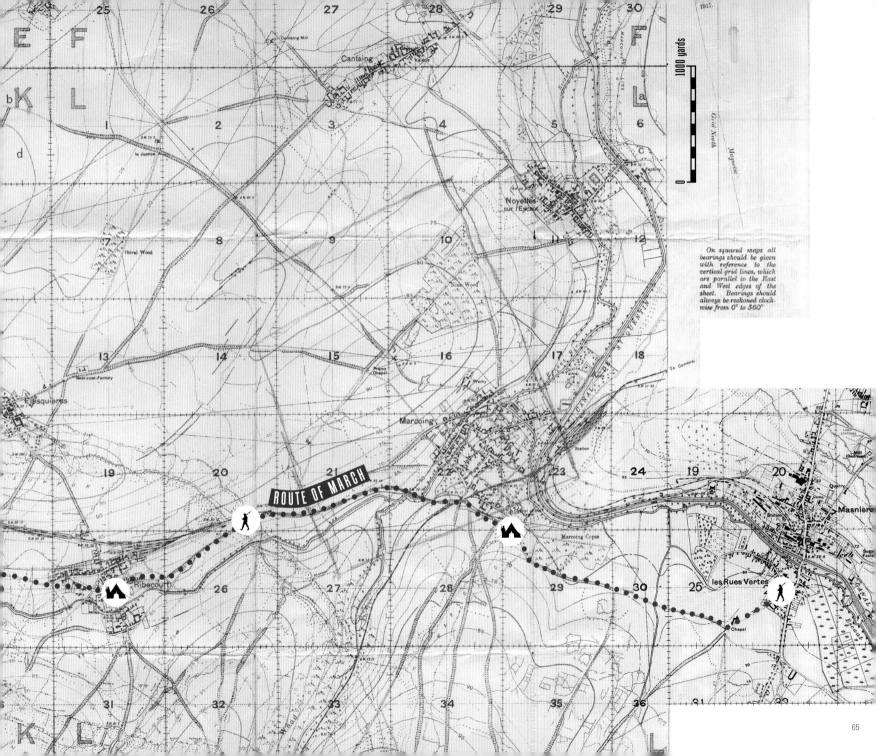

ROUTE OF MARCH

On squared maps all bearings should be given with reference to the vertical grid lines, which are parallel to the East and West edges of the sheet. Bearings should always be reckoned clockwise from 0° to 360°.

1000 yards

Grid North

Magnetic

CHAPTER 5
COUNTER ATTACK
MASNIÈRES AND LES RUES VERTES

1917 3RD DECEMBER

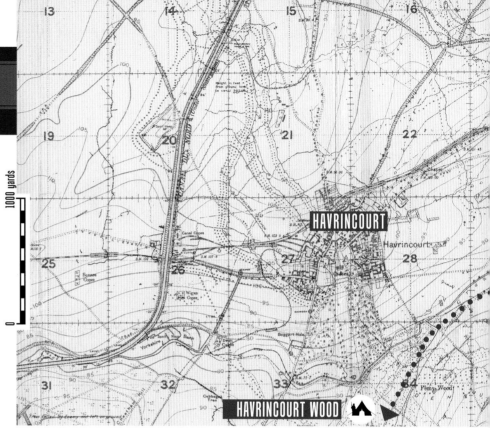

HAVRINCOURT

HAVRINCOURT WOOD

"We walked about 5 miles that evening before reaching this village. The Officers had lost their way, as the next day we found out that it was only 20 minutes walk. The remainder of the night we slept in a barn, and when morning came we had to move away in quick time, as old Jerry was shelling the place. So we went further back and stayed in a trench along a main road, this being on the 3rd Dec. 1917.

Then in the evening we started for another march. We marched along a main road where there were plenty traffic going to and fro so we had to walk in single file each side of the road. Then we marched to our rest camp for the night, in a wood, not even a tent to go inside, just a blanket a man. This was a very pleasant joke, with everything being frozen and of course the weather very cold. So we began making beds under the trees for the night, sleeping six chaps together. The next morning as soon as we was up there was a nice breakfast for us and we soon started on the march again. We arrived at Fins, the village where we started from for the battle. At this place we had huts to go in, and here a good many Guernsey boys joined us, who had lost their way when we left battle. The ones that was with us went back with their regiments. The boys looked rough, but after having a shave and wash we began looking as A.1, this being my first shave for two weeks.

Then the next morning we marched to the station where we got back in cattle trucks and arrived at a place called Houvin, France, this being on the 6th Dec 1917. We was in a poor state as we had heart knocked out of us. We spent a very good time at this place and started to forget what had passed. One day while I was at this place I happened to be at the canteen at the time when two chaps was at the counter. One of them I knew well, and this one asked me how my brother was, so I told him the news. It happened that the other chap was the one that buried my brother, and I was very pleased to hear that he had got buried. He also told me that the Officer that had my brother's belongings had been killed, so things was lost."

1000 yards

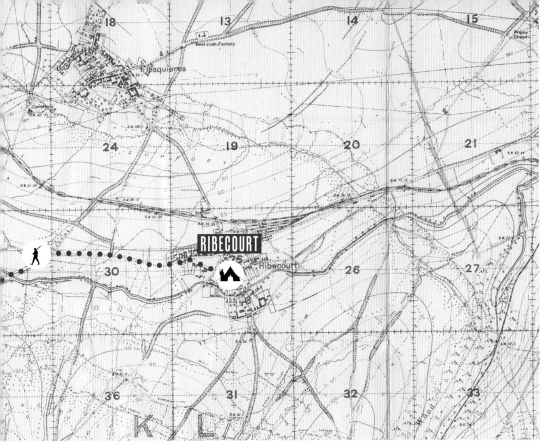

RIBECOURT

of Ribecourt and waited in the trenches until darkness fell, exactly as described by Private le Poidevin, before marching to Havrincourt Wood where they stayed for the night. The following day at 13.00 the Battalion marched to Fins ("the village where we started for the battle"), arriving at 16.00 and were billeted there for the night.

Accounts of the battle show that the 29th Division's stand on the 1st of December 1917 had created a 1,000 yard (900m) salient that could not be held as it was surrounded by the enemy on three sides. So on that night they were ordered to give it up and straighten the line. Battalion Movement Orders state that at 00.45 on the 2nd of December the RGLI "successfully withdrew from Masnières". Fighting continued in the area until the 4th of December but the Guernsey Battalion was too depleted to be involved. Their War Diary shows that at 17.00 on the 2nd of December they marched to Ribecourt, a distance of some 7 km (or just under 5 miles) where they were billeted for the night. They then marched out

At 13.15 on the 5th of December the RGLI marched to Etricourt, where they entrained at 15.00, arriving at "the detraining station" at 04.00 on the 6th of December. The men then marched from the station to Houvin, where they went into billets for "rest, refitting and training". They had marched a total distance of about 25 miles (40 km) in those four days following the battle. Houvin was the place where Private Le Poidevin met the man who had buried his brother. He noted that he was pleased that his brother had a proper burial even though his belongings were lost when the Officer who had them was then killed in action. Herbert Le Poidevin's grave must then have been lost at a later stage, as he is now listed on the Cambrai Memorial at Louverval.

DOING THEIR
DUTY

The Guernsey Star of the 17th of December 1917 carried a letter from the Commanding Officer of the 29th Division, General de Lisle, to the Bailiff of Guernsey, which was read out in the island's Royal Court. It said:

"I want to convey to the Guernsey authorities my very high appreciation of the valuable services rendered by the Royal Guernsey Light Infantry in the battle of Cambrai. Theirs was a wonderful performance. Their first action was on November 20th and though their task on that day was not severe, they carried out all they were asked to do with a completeness that pleased me much. The C.O., de la Condamine, was then invalided and I placed my most experienced C.O. in command. This was Lt Colonel Hart-Synnot, nephew of Sir Reginald Hart.

On November 30th, when the Germans in their heavy surprise attack pierced our line to the south of my sector, the enemy entered the village of Les Rues Vertes, a suburb of Masnières, which suburb was my right flank. It was the Guernsey Light Infantry which recovered this village twice by counter attacks, and which maintained the southern defences of Masnières for two days against seven German attacks with superior forces and very superior artillery. When we were ordered to evacuate

Masnières on the night of December 1st, it being a dangerous salient with the enemy on three sides, it was the Royal Guernsey Light Infantry who covered the withdrawal. Guernsey has every reason to feel the greatest pride in her sons, and I am proud to have them under me fighting alongside my staunch veterans of three years' fighting experience. Many officers and men greatly distinguished themselves, among whom I may first mention Le Bas, and after him Stranger, Stone and Sangster.

I enclose a copy of the Special Order, and feel that Guernsey should participate in the pride we all feel in having done our duty. I regret the casualties of the Battalion were heavy, a further proof if any were needed that they fought magnificently."

The men mentioned by General de Lisle were duly rewarded. Captain Herbert Arthur Le Bas was awarded the Military Cross for his bravery.[25] His citation read "For conspicuous gallantry and devotion to duty. When in command of his own company and men of other units whom he had collected, he held a bridge-head for a day and a night under very heavy fire, keeping his men together by his courage and splendid example, and when the withdrawal was ordered he formed a screen behind which the remainder of the Brigade withdrew." Second Lieutenant

> **"**
>
> *Guernsey has every reason to feel the greatest pride in her sons, and I am proud to have them under me...*

E.J. Stone and Lt Harry Stranger's M.C. citations appear in the same edition of *the London Gazette*. However Battalion casualty lists and CWGC records for the 1st December 1917 show that casualties were indeed heavy with 86 men of the 1st (Service) Battalion, Royal Guernsey Light Infantry, being killed in action on that one day, and more than 300 more were wounded, missing or taken prisoner of war. Of these 70 have no known grave and are commemorated on the Cambrai Memorial at Louverval in Northern France.

The Third Army as a whole reported losses of dead, wounded and missing of approximately 44,000 between the 20th of November and the 8th of December 1917. Of these, some 6,000 were taken prisoner by the Germans on the 30th of November. German losses have been estimated at between 45,000 and 55,000 with 10,000 taken prisoner during the first attack. Almost 40% of the RGLI's total strength was listed as casualties over that period. Losses were so great that if these men could not be replaced the Battalion would have had to be disbanded, so the Lieutenant Governor, Sir Reginald Hart, went to the War Office for help. As a result of this about 200 men from the 3rd Battalion the North Staffordshire Regiment who were stationed in Guernsey were drafted into the RGLI.

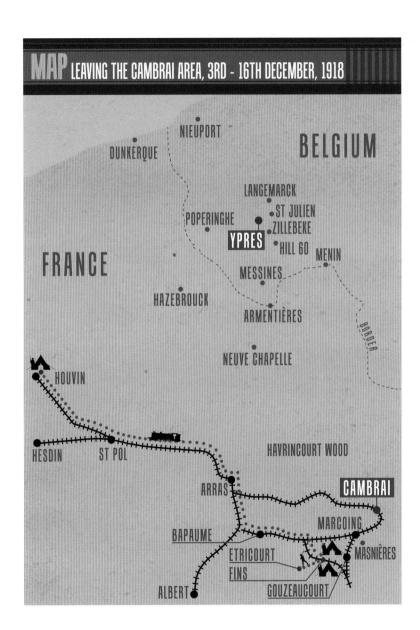

MAP LEAVING THE CAMBRAI AREA, 3RD - 16TH DECEMBER, 1918

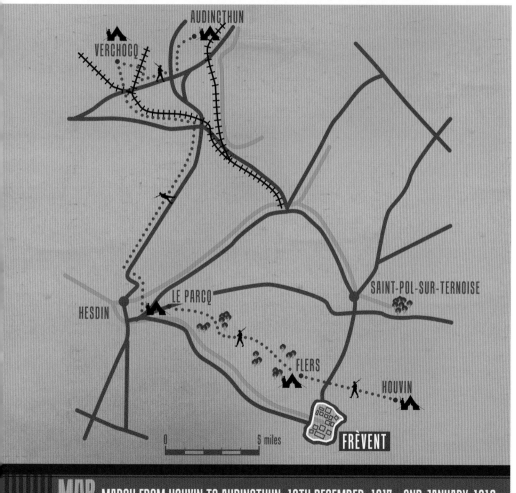

MAP MARCH FROM HOUVIN TO AUDINGTHUN, 16TH DECEMBER, 1917 - 2ND JANUARY, 1918

1917 16TH DECEMBER

" On the 16th of Dec 1917 we left this village for another place and had a three days march before us. The first day was fine, only the last mile it began snowing just before the dark was upon us, and we rested in a village called Flers. The next morning we started on our march having a nice white path to walk upon. The next evening we rested at Le Parcq, and the third day's march was awful as the top of the snow was frozen, so we had a job to walk along. Then the village we got billeted to was called Verchocq, Dec 18th 1917. At this place we spent our Xmas and New Year, and at the time we left this place there was still snow about, this being on the 3rd Jan 1918. We got billeted in another village called Audincthun, near St-Pol. It was at this place that our Officer received Military Distinction. This was the report given: "Lieutenant H.E.K. Stranger of the First Service Battalion Royal Guernsey Light Infantry, he held an important bridgehead, during a period of strenuous fighting at close quarters. He collected and organised men of several units, and held the bridge successfully against the enemy efforts to break through. He set a splendid example of courage and determination." I was one of them that won this distinction for him."

To wish You a very happy Christmas

« A merry Christmas ! Everything's as right as rain ! »

GREETINGS

« Remember the day, Bill : Let's make these look
a bit cheerful ! »

Happy New Year

« Merry Christmas ! here's
looking at you ! »

Greetings

« I feel like Father Christmas
wi hout the wiskers ! »

HAPPY CHRISTMAS

The same to you,
and many of them !

A Merry
Xmas

« I don't want it myself : and besides, it makes
a fine Xmas gift for my country ! »

ALL GOOD WISHES

« Merry Christmas ! The compliments of the season ! »

Selection of original WW1 Christmas and New
Year Cards. From the series entitled 'Sketches
of Tommy's Life' by Fergus Mackain.
Circa 1917-1918.
GMAG 1993.108

The remnants of the RGLI
only had a brief opportunity to
recuperate after the disastrous
events of Cambrai. Battalion
records show that on the 16th
of December the RGLI did
indeed march to Flers, where
they were billeted for the night,
after which they marched to
Le Parcq, where they also
stayed for one night. They then
marched to Verchocq which
was to the North West of the
main battlefields and away
from the Front Lines, where
they went into billets. Later
in 1918 Winston Churchill
was to stay at the Château
of Verchocq. Weather across
Europe in December 1917 was
particularly cold with snow,
which Channel Islanders rarely
see at home.

PARADES AND
AWARDS

Lieutenant Colonel
T.L. de Havilland, Commanding
Officer RGLI. Circa 1918.
The Barry Jones Collection. © Guernsey Museum.

The RGLI remained at Verchocq for training from the 19th of December 1917 to the 2nd of January 1918. The Battalion Diary notes that there was a Brigade Ceremonial Parade on the 11th of January. Here Lieutenant Colonel de Havilland was awarded the D.S.O. and Major J.A.Walbeoffe Wilson, M.C., of the Middlesex regiment but on attachment to the RGLI, received a second bar to his M.C.. Lieutenants H.E.K. Stranger and E.J. Stone both received the Military Cross, and Sergeants W.H. Budden and W.J. Le Poidevin (no relation) received the Distinguished Conduct Medal.

The Distinguished Conduct medal was a second level decoration for bravery, awarded to Other Ranks of the British Army, whilst the Military Cross was a third level decoration awarded to Officers. The citation[26] for Captain Harry Easterbrook Knollys Stranger, the officer mentioned by Private Le Poidevin, noted that he "…held an important bridgehead, during a period of strenuous fighting at close quarters. He collected and organised men of several units, and held the bridge successfully against the enemy efforts to break through. He set a splendid example of courage and determination." This matches almost word for word with Private Le Poidevin's account.

Two days after this parade, Reinforcement 5, consisting of 50 Other Ranks, joined the Battalion at Base Depot.[27] Parks notes that Reinforcements 4 and 6 consisted mainly of trained men, some 170 in total, who were formerly in the North Staffordshire regiment, which was stationed in Guernsey at the time but does not mention the origins of Reinforcement 5. They were probably a mix of men from the 2nd (Reserve) Battalion, RGLI and the North Staffs Regiment. Because of the large number of casualties suffered at Cambrai and the limited number of reserves available from the small population of the Bailiwick, as time went on soldiers from other units were drafted in. This meant that many who fought with the RGLI in later battles were not Channel Islanders. These reinforcements were usually drafted into the 2nd (Reserve) Battalion based in Guernsey, then sent to France after training as they were needed. Some trained men such as those from the North Staffordshire Regiment joined the 1st (Service) Battalion directly.

As soon as the men were rested and numbers built up again the RGLI was on the move once more. Private Le Poidevin notes:

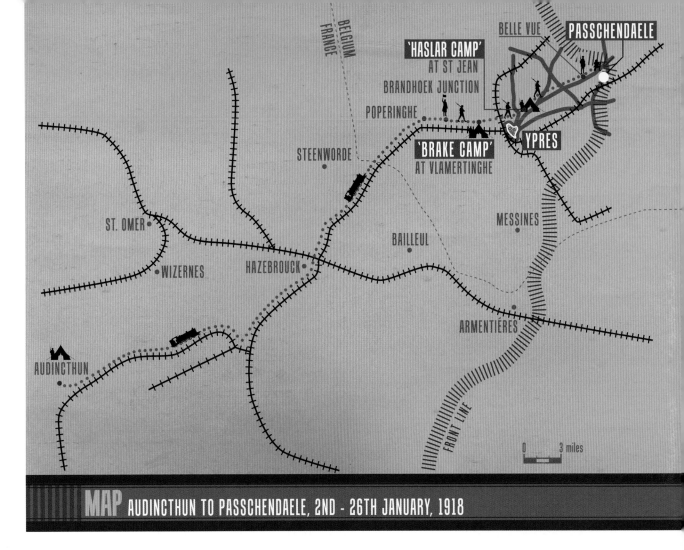

MAP AUDINCTHUN TO PASSCHENDAELE, 2ND - 26TH JANUARY, 1918

16TH JANUARY 1918

" *The snow cleared away the day before leaving, this being the 16th of January. We marched along to a station nearby, which was in France and took a train which was bound for Belgium. On our way we passed Poperinghe and got down at Broodhoek (sic) Junction, and marched for Brake camp. After staying a day in the camp we left and got billeted closer to the line, in Haslar camp on the Ypres front, and on the 18th January 1918 the Battalion went for the line. I was moved the other side to English camp and joined our company which had taken over reserve line at Bellevue on Passchendale on the 19th January 1918.*

In the day all we could see was nothing but shells holes and dead here and there."

1918 22ND JANUARY

British casualties lying amongst German barbed wire entanglements after a British attack, 1918.
E 3149. © Imperial War Museums.

" It wasn't safe to walk about day time, Gerry [28] used to shell this place very often, and not very pleasant at times. Life was very sweet when in danger. And on the 22nd January we left reserve line to relieve B Company in the front line. This evening it was lovely moon light and we were in danger of the enemy spotting us going up. In going up that night we lost our way. The way that troops got in front trenches, was by means of a white tape laid down, but we missed the tape and was driving for Gerry lines. But as it happened one turned back and found the tape. So when we got in the front trench, our gun team was sent in an advance post in front of the trench. This place was made out of two shells holes and two or three times while we were in this place our guns had put on short range which almost put us out of action. This evening, when we was on our way to this advance post I was hidden in a shell hole waiting for my turn to get across. In the same shell hole was another chap of some other regiment waiting for a chance to get across to his regiment. When I saw everything clear I got up to cross, which he did the same, and at the same time Gerry opened fire which

"Gerry opened fire which hit this chap killing him on the spot, a very close shave for myself."

TERRIBLE
CONDITIONS

hit this chap killing him on the spot, a very close shave for myself.

One day as we was looking over we could see about 12 men standing up near Gerry's line, then we came to see that some of our boys was speaking to Gerry. When we saw this we thought the war must be over, so the next day our boys saw the Gerries coming towards their trench, and instead of speaking, it was a few bombs which killed a few of our boys. Old Gerry wasn't long before having the trick upon him. Then the night came when we got relieved, and had the order that as soon as we was relieved to go right back past the wood road and wait there for the remainder of the Battalion. This we done but in going down three or four shells busted just over us, we happened lucky as only one got wounded. This was on the 26th Jan 1918. This evening we went right back to Brake camp, and from this camp the Battalion went on different fatigues."

The Battalion War Diary again confirms Private Le Poidevin's recollections, noting that on the 16th of January they marched to Wizernes (which is in the Pas de Calais department of Northern France but very close to the Belgian border) where they entrained for Brandhoek in Belgium. They went into Brake camp overnight before marching to St Jean where they went into Haslar Camp.

Operational orders for the 18th and 19th of January state that "2 Royal Fusiliers and the 1 RGLI will take over the right section of the Divisional Front tonight 18/19th inst. from the 2 Royal Berkshires (Front Line) and the 1st Royal Irish Rifles (Reserve Line). The residue of the Companies will remain behind at ENGLISH FARM C.2.7.B Central under command of Capt. Hutchinson, they will relieve men of their own Companies periodically in the front and reserve trenches and will be used for carrying up rations."

The official reports do not mention that the men lost their way and were heading for the wrong lines. Many other accounts mention that white marker tape was laid on the ground after dusk to lead the troops through the maze of trenches and shell holes to the correct place on the front line.

Some idea of the cold and miserable conditions the men had to endure in this section of the line is shown by the continuation of this Order, which noted that "... Every man going into the trenches will wear leather or fur jerkins, 2 sandbags round each leg instead of puttees, gum boots, P.H. helmets and box respirators in the alert position and every other man will carry a shovel... All men going up the line will take 3 pairs of dry socks. Men at ENGLISH FARM will treat their feet properly before going up to relieve men in the line."

TRENCH
FOOT

Every entry in the Operational Orders at this stage mentions treatment of the feet. Trench Foot was a common ailment caused by cold, wet and insanitary conditions. In the trenches men stood for hours on end on soil without being able to remove wet socks or boots. Their feet would gradually go numb and the skin would turn red or blue. If untreated, trench foot could turn gangrenous and the only treatment then was amputation. It was a particular problem in the early stages of the war, with over 20,000 men in the British Army being treated for it during the winter of 1914-15. By 1917 there were standard procedures to attempt to reduce the problem. Soldiers were ordered to dry their feet and change their socks several times a day, taking three pairs of socks with them into the trenches. As well as drying their feet, they were sometimes told to cover them with grease made from whale-oil to act as a barrier against the water.

A British officer wading through thigh-deep mud in a British trench in December 1916.
E 577. © Imperial War Museums.

Trench Foot was not the only peril soldiers had to contend with even when they were away from the Front Line. Battalion Casualty Lists show that men were still being lost on an almost daily basis. Parks states that "Sniping and trench raids were common, resulting in a steady trickle of casualties." Trench raids were small scale surprise attacks on enemy positions. Typically, raids were carried out at night by small teams of men who would often black up their faces before crossing the barbed wire and shell holes of no man's land to infiltrate the enemy's trench systems. The distance between friendly and enemy front lines varied from several hundred metres down to under a hundred metres and raids were conducted by both sides in order to gain intelligence. The generals believed it also boosted the fighting spirits of the men who could become disheartened after hours of inactivity in a cold and muddy trench, but the main result was a constant trickle of casualties. The trick played on the RGLI by the Germans probably happened on the 24th of January, as Battalion Casualty Lists show that four men were killed in action on that day but none were wounded. As a result of all these further losses RGLI numbers needed a further boost so on the 24th of January 70 men, mainly former members of

the 3rd Battalion North Staffordshire Regiment, joined as Reinforcement 6.

Almost as soon as this reinforcement arrived, Relief Orders note that "The Battalion will be relieved on the night of the 26th/27th January in the right sector of the Brigade front by the 1st Newfoundland Regiment in the right subsector and the 2nd Hants Regt. in the left subsector and will proceed to the BRANDHOEK area." The Battalion War Diary shows that on the 26th of January A and B Companies marched from California Camp to Brake Camp, Brandhoek, whilst C and D Companies entrained at Weltje and arrived at Brake Camp at 4 a.m. on 27th. An ambulance was provided to pick up any men who were incapable of marching the full distance. Once they were settled at Brake Camp, cleaning up and training continued until the end of the month.

After two months of fighting and moving around, the men of the RGLI found themselves posted back to the area where they had been on fatigues during the previous autumn, which must have made them feel that the events of Cambrai had been a dreadful waste of life.

RETURN TO PASSCHENDAELE

Map labels:
- 'HASLAR CAMP'
- 'JUNCTION CAMP'
- 'RED ROSE CAMP' AT SPREE FARM
- PASSCHENDAELE RIDGE
- PASSCHENDAELE
- St JULIEN
- ABRAHAM HEIGHTS
- BELGIUM / FRANCE
- BRANDHOEK JUNCTION
- St JEAN
- POPERINGHE
- 'BRAKE CAMP' AT VLAMERTINGHE
- YPRES
- ZONNEBEKE
- STEENVOORDE
- GODEWAERSVELDE
- MESSINES RIDGE
- BAILLEUL
- HAZEBROUCK
- STEENWERCK
- ARMENTIÈRES
- FRONT LINE
- 0 3 miles

MAP ANTI-AIRCRAFT DUTY, 26TH JANUARY - 8TH MARCH, 1918

11TH FEBRUARY 1918

Private Le Poidevin goes on to say:

" Our gun team left this camp the next day and went on anti-air craft in Abraham's Heights right near Bethleem Farm on Passchendale. We did not have many shells at this place. We left this place on the 11th Feb, and joined the Battalion at California camp and took the train for Poperinghe and our company was billeted in the town in the street called La Rue-L'Hospital near La Grande Place. From this place every morning we took the train and went up towards the line on fatigue, getting brought back every evening by train. We left Poperinghe on the 19th of Feb for Steenwerck in France. Here we was right out of the noise of the guns, we were billeted in a barn in the village called Steenwerck-de-La-Copelet. We stayed here for a rest, leaving this place on the 7th of March and marched to a station called Godewaersvelde, got on the train passing Poperinghe and got off at Broodhoek Junction Belgium, for Red Rose camp. The same day our gun team was sent on Anti Air craft on Ypres main road, left this place the next day the 8th and joined the Battalion at Irish camp doing fatigue behind reserve line day time."

WORKING
PARTIES

"

Here we was right out of the noise of the guns"

The Battalion Diary notes that on the 3rd of February the Battalion relieved the King's Own Scottish Borderers at English Camp, where it was employed on working parties which consisted mostly of digging defences and wiring. Relief Orders for the same date note that: "... The 1st RGLI will relieve the 1 King's Own SB's (Scottish Borderers) in English Camp... The Battalion will be formed up ready to move off on the road outside the Camp at 1.45 p.m.....One Lewis Gun and team of 6 per Company will proceed with one Lewis Gun Limber to the relief of four anti-aircraft guns of the 1 King's Own Scottish Borderers." Private Le Poidevin was a Lewis gunner so presumably "our gun team" was the team of six from his Company. On the 6th of February Reinforcement 7, a small reinforcement consisting of just 15 men joined the RGLI at their camp. The Battalion then moved to Haslar camp on the 9th of February where they continued with the working parties. Then on the 11th of February they were relieved by the 2nd Royal Fusiliers, after which they

went by train from Wieltje to Poperinghe where they went into billets. From the 12th to the 18th of February three Companies were employed on trenching and draining in the forward area, entraining daily at Poperinghe and returning each evening at about 5pm. They then moved to the Eêcke area on the 19th of February, where they went into billets where they remained until early March. On the 21st of February they were joined by Reinforcement 8, consisting of 60 Other Ranks. On the 27th of February there was a Battalion ceremonial parade, where ribbons were presented to Captain H.E.K. Stranger, M.C., Lieutenant E.J. Stone, M.C., 843 Cpl J. Sealley, M.M., 841 Pte T.R. Robin, M.M. and 610 Pte C.J. Yeaghers, MM.

There was only one casualty reported during the whole of this period. This period of relative quiet did not last for long, however.

Private Le Poidevin goes on to say:

1918 13TH MARCH

" One day on arriving at our camp from work, we noticed that the place had been shelled while we had been gone. That day we had just been dismissed when a shell came and hit one of our tents, no one in at the time, we did not sleep quiet that night. The next day being the 14th of March old Gerry started with his long range guns to shell this camp, which was about 7 miles from the front line. This meant that we had to move from this place so three companies went to California camp and our company to Junction camp a little ways off. In this camp we were billeted in huts.

The next day being the 15th, we went down to Vlamertinge for baths, being carried in motors lorries there and back. On our way back we saw 5 horses laid out just been killed by a shell. From this place we went on fatigue along No.5. track, which was over 7 miles long. Besides this there were different tracks, some much longer.

We left this camp on the 17th of March 1918 for the line."

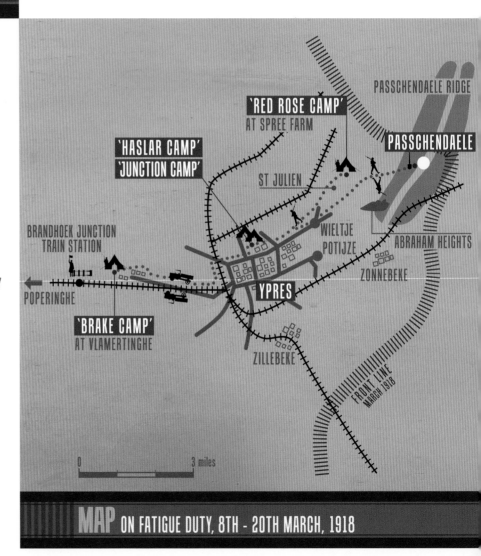

PASSCHENDAELE RIDGE
'RED ROSE CAMP' AT SPREE FARM
PASSCHENDAELE
'HASLAR CAMP'
'JUNCTION CAMP'
ST JULIEN
BRANDHOEK JUNCTION TRAIN STATION
WIELTJE
POTIJZE
ABRAHAM HEIGHTS
ZONNEBEKE
POPERINGHE
YPRES
'BRAKE CAMP' AT VLAMERTINGHE
ZILLEBEKE
FRONT LINE MARCH 1918
0   3 miles

MAP ON FATIGUE DUTY, 8TH - 20TH MARCH, 1918

we were wearing our box respirators, as old Gerry was sending over gas."

left
British soldiers at a supply depot loading ammunition boxes onto pack ponies bound for the Reserve Line. Artist's impression by Brian Byron, 2009.
GMAG 2009.175. © Guernsey Museum.

below
Men of the RGLI practicing with small box respirators during their training in Guernsey. Circa 1917.

The Barry Jones Collection. © Guernsey Museum.

"Going up we went along the wooden road and passed Paellerve which was reserve line, our company taking over support line, A and B company front line, D company reserve. Our work night time was carrying rations from reserve line up to the front line, as every evening the pack ponies brought up rations as far as reserve.

On the 19th of March the Germans came over the top, A and B company had many casualties. The next evening our company went and relieved A company, this being on the 20th of March. This evening in going up we were wearing our box respirators, as old Gerry was sending over gas."

1918 21ST MARCH

" *This turn going in front line our platoon only had one N.C.O. which meant me taking charge of the Lewis gun team, so as soon as we arrived I took over our post. Next to mine was a bombing section. In this trench was nothing but mud and in some places one was obliged to catch hold of each side of the trench to be able to pass through. The same evening they were sending over trench mortars, just below our trench, which killed six of our chaps. As the Germans had raided this trench the night before, we were on a good look out for fear they came over. During the first night the Germans kept very quiet, no Verey lights being sent up by them. I found that strange, I thought there was something on the move. That evening I was in a kind of a fix as the few Verey lights I had was damp. The day light arrived and nothing happened so after keeping awake all night we slept in turn during the day. The next night I took good care and had good Verey lights. Then as soon as night was upon us we started arranging our trench and the Officer came around with the rum. This gave us heart to get on with work. After midnight old Gerry began sending over rifle grenades but we were lucky that they couldn't reach us, but they wounded a few at the lower end of the trench. Now and again shells were pitching, so during night time we never had a minute's rest.*

The third night being the worst night of all, we were kept on the move and they kept on sending trench mortars over, and just before day break they put one just in the corner of our trench, killing the two sentries of the bombing section and wounding two of them, this being a close shave for us. Then after this we were left alone. Around our trenches were many shell holes which was full of

far left
German infantrymen in
a well-appointed trench
preparing to fire rifle
grenades at the British lines.
Circa 1914-1918.

left
Allied troops following
a wooden duckboard
'track' laid through a mass
of mud, shell holes and
dead trees laid waste by
artillery bombardment.
Passchendaele, July 1917.

water. These trench mortars was falling so thick that they were joining these shell holes together with the trenches, making it ten times worse for mud for us. Now the next night was our last night and we were longing for the time to come, and yet there was this trench to put up in which the trench mortar fell. First of all we had to pick up the two dead bodies. We wrapped them up in oil sheets and placed them on top of the trench, then did up this trench ready for our relief. Then when the relief came, this being on the 24th March, we had to wait along side of the company head quarters for the remainder of the company then we marched for the duck boards on our way for a rest camp. The same evening, arriving at California camp, we always looked for a cup of tea as there was no way of having any while in the trenches, only what we made ourselves and no water but shell hole water."

DIRE
CONDITIONS

This account shows that they were not only in danger when they were in the front line, and Battalion Casualty Lists confirm that losses occurred on an almost daily basis. More than 30 men were killed in action during this period, while many more were wounded, gassed or taken prisoner of war. By this stage the German army had developed very long range artillery, such as the gun that shelled Paris from over 120 km (75 miles) away. Thus the camps where the fatigue parties were based were close enough to be easy targets for the Germans. Also Private Le Poidevin's graphic description of conditions in this sector is well documented elsewhere. The divisional historian[29] describing the sector wrote, "The defences consisted of shallow slits without communications and without wire. The dead of friends and foes still lay unburied and supporting lines or reserve positions did not exist... The work of preparing defences was exceptionally arduous. The whole area had been churned up by shells into craters which were full of water, and in some places these craters were overlapping and the soil like a morass." The "wooden road" Private Le Poidevin refers to consisted of duckboards, wooden planks laid over the mud which were the only way of crossing the churned up and waterlogged terrain.

The Verey lights that he mentions were flares fired from a pistol and were used for signalling and illumination but each flare only lasted for about 10 seconds. He also says that their officer came round with rum during the night. As part of their standard ration soldiers on duty were allowed 1/2 gill (about 70 ml.) of rum per week, to be given at the discretion of the commanding general. A single pub measure is 25 ml, so it was a good tot, meant to lift the spirits of the men.

Official records show that on the 17th of March the Battalion finished its turn of fatigue duties and relieved the 1st Lancashire Fusiliers in the Poelcapelle sector of the front line. The Battalion Relief orders confirm Private Le Poidevin's reference to their night work, noting that "… 5% of the Support Company will be employed nightly on carrying Royal Engineers material from MOSSELMARKT to the Front Company's Headquarters. The Reserve Company will furnish ration parties. 25% of the Reserve Company will be at the disposal of the Tunnelling Company nightly." They had relieved the 1st Lancashire Fusiliers on the 17th of March and remained in the Poelcapelle sector of the line until they were relieved by the 2nd Battalion Royal Fusiliers on the 23rd. Meanwhile they were joined on the 19th of March

"many chaps went off for hospital"

by Reinforcement 9, the last men to join the Service Battalion and see action. This reinforcement included for the first time "a significant number"[30] of RGLI men who had previously been invalided home following injuries or illness whilst on service but were now considered to be fighting fit again.

Private Le Poidevin describes men being gassed and a trench mortar landing near them and killing six men on the 20th of March. Battalion Casualty lists show that several men were gassed on the 19th and 20th of March. However although the same lists show three men as being killed in action on the 20th, the Commonwealth War Graves Commission does not list any RGLI men as having been killed in action on that date. There are other minor anomalies between the information given by these two sources for this period, though overall figures match up and between them fit with Private Le Poidevin's account of events. He continues:

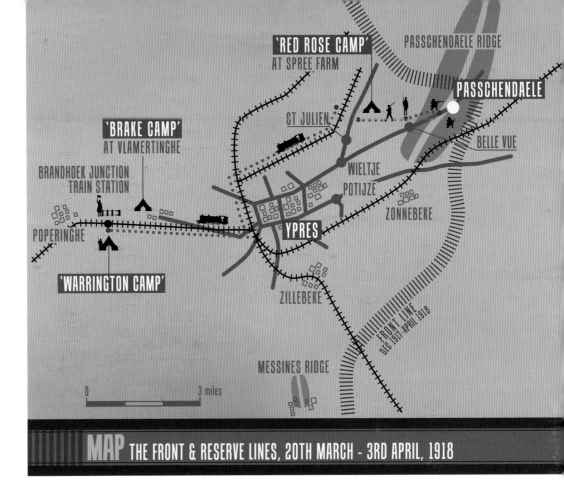

MAP THE FRONT & RESERVE LINES, 20TH MARCH - 3RD APRIL, 1918

27TH MARCH 1918

" This camp being in range of the guns we were wishing to be moved further on, but instead we got moved up the line, this being 27th March our company taking over reserve line at Bellevue, Passchendale, Belgium. While we were at California camp, many chaps went off for hospital, being slightly gassed and the strength of our platoon going for the line was 17 men. So like this, being in reserve we had double work. We spent three days and most of this time it was raining. We were wet through from the time we went in till the time we came out, getting relieved on the 30th March."

1918 30TH MARCH

" *From Bellevue we went down to Wavelgem Junction near Spree farm. We marched in groups and as each group arrived at Spree farm the cooks was there waiting for the men from the line with warm tea. As every man had his tea in turn we got up in a train that was near, then waited for the remainder of boys, before starting. But worst luck, old Gerry began shelling this place, placing them each side of this train and before many minutes a shell hit right upon one of the cookers, killing seven men and two horses. The train wasn't long before being put on the move after this. The remainder of the boys had to get to the camp the best they could.*

We got billeted in Warrington camp near the town of Ypres, and on the 3rd of April we left for the line again. We were carried on the light railway till Wieltje Junction, and from there on the duck boards for the line. This was one of my longest walk on the duck boards, I thought we'd never reach the front line. This time we were more on the right of Passchendale near Hill 60. Our company took over front line. This part was a very lonely and rough place, and the four days we spent there was very quiet. We got relieved on the 7th of April 1918, and had our march along the duck boards then took the train at Wieltje Junction for Warrington camp, Ypres, reaching Warrington camp on the 8th of April."

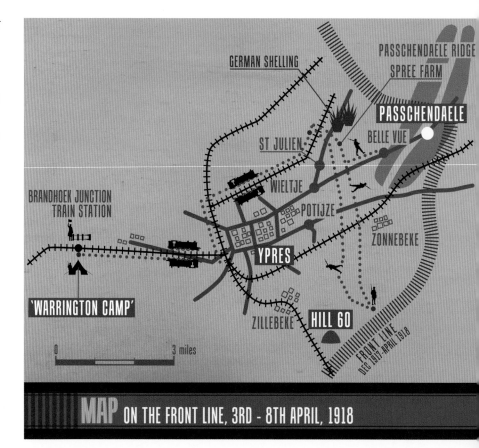

MAP ON THE FRONT LINE, 3RD - 8TH APRIL, 1918

REST AND
TRAINING

The Battalion Diary again confirms Private Le Poidevin's account of his whereabouts over this period, stating that on the 27th of March the RGLI relieved the 1st Lancashire Fusiliers in the left sector of the Brigade front. They were based at California Camp at this stage. It then reports that on the 29th of March the Battalion was relieved by the 1st Border Regiment and proceeded to Warrington camp for rest and training, where they stayed until the 1st of April. Relief Orders note that "...86 Brigade will be relieved by 87 Brigade in the Right Sector of the Divisional front on the night of the 30th to 31st inst. The Battalion will be relieved by the 1st Border Regiment and will proceed to RED ROSE CAMP...Companies will on relief proceed to SPREE FARM where they will entrain for BRANDHOEK. First train leaves at midnight. The trains will be filled up as Units arrive. On arrival at BRANDHOEK Companies will march independently to RED ROSE CAMP. Hot tea will be arranged for by the Quartermaster at the entraining point." Tea was obviously an important comfort for the men as it features several times in Private Le Poidevin's account. Like the rum and cigarette rations, it was thought to be vital in maintaining morale, and a hot drink would have been especially welcome in the cold, wet conditions. Private Le Poidevin notes that his platoon consisted of 17 men at this stage. At that date a full strength British platoon should have around 50 men, led by a Lieutenant. He was usually assisted by a senior Non-Commissioned Officer, the platoon Sergeant.

Private Le Poidevin notes that from the 3rd to the 7th of April the Battalion was based near Hill 60. In order to get to the lines they went by light railway as far as Wieltje Junction, then had to walk to the front line. They were met by guides when they got off the train, and Battalion Operational orders note that they had to go via Judah Track, which meant walking on duckboards again. Soldiers who stepped off them would just have sunk into the waterlogged ground. The RGLI relieved the Argyll and Sutherland Highlanders on the 3rd of April and were relieved by the 12th East Surrey Regiment on the 7th.

Private Le Poidevin describes Hill 60 as a "very lonely and rough place." It lies to the south of Zillebeke, and was much fought over as it had excellent views over much of Ypres and the front line around it. It was not a natural hill but was formed by the spoil excavated when a cutting was created for the Ypres to Comines railway.

HILL 60

Nowadays Hill 60 carries a plaque which says:

Hill 60, the scene of bitter fighting was held by German troops from the 16th December 1914 to the 7th April 1915 when it was captured after the explosion of five mines by the British 5th Division. On the following 5th May it was recaptured by the German XV Corps. It remained in German hands until the battle of Messines on the 7th June 1917 when after many months of underground fighting two mines were exploded here and at the end of April 1918 after the battles of the Lys it passed into German hands again. It was finally retaken by British troops under the command of H.M. King of the Belgians on the 28th September 1918. In the broken tunnels beneath this enclosure many British and German dead were buried and the hill is therefore preserved so far as nature will permit in the state in which it was left after the Great War.

On the 7th of April the Battalion was relieved by the 12th East Surrey Regiment and went by train from Borry Farm (where tea was again provided) to Warrington Camp where they went into billets. Relief Orders note that "... On arrival in Camp, all men will wash their feet in water, which will be provided by the Quartermaster. Company Commanders will ensure that this process is inspected by platoon." This again shows the importance of foot care, especially in the wet conditions that they had endured in this sector. The one good thing about this period is that there were no casualties, though there were several in the previous few weeks with many men being killed or injured when they were not on front line duties.

"
On arrival in Camp, all men will wash their feet in water"

right
British soldiers in a trench attending to the constant demands of wet feet and the threat of vermin. Artist's impression by Brian Byron, 2009.
GMAG 2009.175. © Guernsey Museum.

CHAPTER 7 **DOULIEU**

1918 9TH APRIL

> Then after a day or two in this camp we heard that the Division was on the move. Then the next order was to pack up, this being on the 9th of April, so during the afternoon we were paraded in fighting order ready to move off. We were bound towards France, as the enemy had broken through and had started to advance. The Battalion was taken in motor lorries. This turn I was put in the 10 percent so I was kept back, leaving this camp the next day, the 9th, and marching to the Division. C wing was where all the 10 percent of every unit in the Division, this being at Road camp near Poperinghe, so between every unit they made a Battalion.
>
> On the 12th of April as we were down the village, the order came that all men of the 28th Division had to go back to their quarters. Then as soon as we got back the orders was to back up and get ready in fighting order as the 29th Division had been cut up, so we had to reinforce them. Then we fell in by companies on the playground. Then we marched for the station where we stayed an hour or two, because something had gone wrong with the train. At last we marched for another station, and by the time we got in the trains it was past mid-night, and we got out about an hour before day break. When marching from this station,

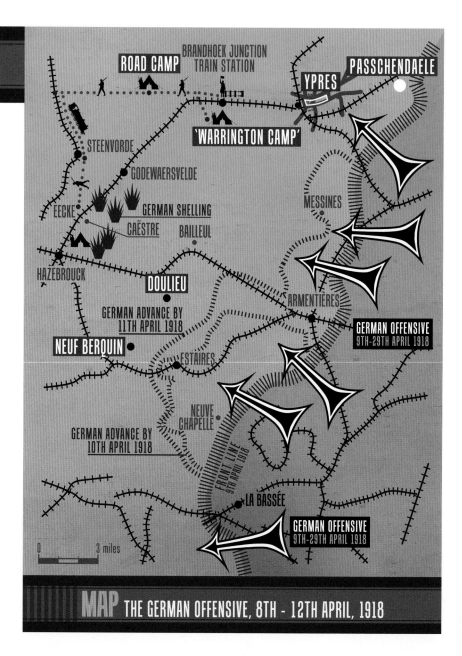

MAP THE GERMAN OFFENSIVE, 8TH - 12TH APRIL, 1918

….a pitiful sight, to see people young and old coming down this main road"

we passed through a town, and we were busy looking around for the name of this place, and in going through the square I noticed a bandstand which I knew very well. The place was called Steenvoorde. We also passed where we used to bath when billeted just outside this place.

The next place was the village of Eêck, and now it was day light we could see nothing but these French wagons loaded, and cattle tied behind. In some of the wagons there were people living. These had come from the front line towards Armentières and La Bassée. Then we halted just outside a village called Caëstre. While we were here the Germans began shelling this village. This was a pitiful sight, to see people young and old coming down this main road getting chased from their homes. Then we heard that the Guernsey Battalion was cut up, so then we were marched past this village in reserve where we stayed till the 29th Division got relieved."

Private Le Poidevin's account of the last days that the RGLI spent at the front is very brief: The Germans opened their Spring Offensive on the 21st of March 1918, knowing that at this stage of the war their only remaining chance of victory was to defeat the Allies before the overwhelming resources of the United States swung into action. The Americans had entered the war in Spring 1917 but had only recently started to deploy significant numbers of troops at the front. The Germans also benefitted from a temporary advantage in numbers as the Russian withdrawal from the war in March 1918 had freed up nearly 50 Divisions.

Four separate attacks made up the Offensive. These were codenamed Michael, Georgette, Gneisenau, and Blücher-Yorck. Michael was the first

attack, launched with the intention of breaking through the Allied lines and outflanking the British forces that held the Front from the Somme to the English Channel. The Germans hoped that the French would be so disheartened by this that they would seek an Armistice. German forces initially achieved an unprecedented advance with British and French trenches being taken by new infiltration tactics. Previous attacks had been characterized by long artillery bombardments and mass assaults. During the Spring Offensive however the German Army used artillery briefly and employed small groups of specially trained lightly armed storm troopers to infiltrate weak points and strike into the vulnerable rear areas. Allied strongpoints were bypassed, to be mopped up by conventional infantry.

OPERATION GEORGETTE

After a few days of success, the German advance began to falter as the infantry became exhausted. Also support in the form of artillery and supplies could not move as fast as the lightly armed units mentioned previously. In addition fresh British and Australian troops were moved into the Amiens area to protect the vital railhead there. Following several fruitless attempts to capture Amiens, the German General Ludendorff called off Operation Michael on the 5th of April, just over a fortnight after it had begun. The Allies had lost some 255,000 men whilst German losses amounted to almost 240,000, many of them from élite storm trooper units. The RGLI had been in the Ypres area of Belgium during this period but their move from Belgium to Northern France on the 9th of April was a result of Operation Michael, which had drawn British forces away from other sectors in order to defend Amiens. The Germans realised that this left the sector including the important rail route through Hazebrouck and the approaches to the Channel ports of Calais, Boulogne and Dunkerque vulnerable.

Operation Georgette was planned to take advantage of this situation and the Germans attacked here on the 9th of April 1918. The main attack was made on the sector defended by the Portuguese Expeditionary Force. Despite a desperate defence in which they lost more than 7,000 men, the Portuguese Army and the British on their northern flank were rapidly overrun. The Germans broke through along 9 miles (about 14km) of the front line and advanced up to 5 miles (8 km) into Allied territory. At their furthest point they reached the town of Estaires on the river Lys, where they were finally halted. British troops on the southern flank also managed to hold the line of La Bassée Canal. The next day the Germans widened their attack to the north, surrounding Armentières and capturing most of the Messines Ridge. By the end of the day, the few British divisions in reserve were hard-pressed to hold a line along the River Lys.

The RGLI Battalion Diary states that on the 9th of April the main body of the Battalion (minus the 10% which included Private Le Poidevin, kept back to join others in a mixed Battalion) went by bus from Brandhoek in Belgium, leaving at 8.30pm and proceeded to Vieux Berquin in Northern France. From here they marched into billets about 1,000 yards (some 900m) west of Neuf Berquin. On the 10th of April, they took up a position in front of Doulieu and dug in for the night beyond the village. The following morning, 11th April, the

Field-Marshal Sir Douglas Haig, Commander-in-Chief of the British Armies in France.

Battalion filled up the gap between the 40th Division on the left and 87th Brigade on the right.

This was the day on which General Haig issued his famous "Backs to the Wall" Order of the Day:

"

There is no other course open to us but to fight it out"

By FIELD-MARSHAL SIR DOUGLAS HAIG
K.T., G.C.B., G.C.V.O., K.C.I.E.
Commander-in-Chief, British Armies in France
To ALL RANKS OF THE BRITISH ARMY IN FRANCE AND FLANDERS
Three weeks ago to-day the enemy began his terrific attacks against us on a fifty-mile front. His objects are to separate us from the French, to take the Channel Ports and destroy the British Army. In spite of throwing already 106 Divisions into the battle and enduring the most reckless sacrifice of human life, he has as yet made little progress towards his goals. We owe this to the determined fighting and self-sacrifice of our troops. Words fail me to express the admiration which I feel for the splendid resistance offered by all ranks of our Army under the most trying circumstances.
Many amongst us now are tired. To those I would say that Victory will belong to the side which holds out the longest. The French Army is moving rapidly and in great force to our support. There is no other course open to us but to fight it out. Every position must be held to the last man: there must be no retirement. With our backs to the wall and believing in the justice of our cause each one of us must fight on to the end. The safety of our homes and the Freedom of mankind alike depend upon the conduct of each one of us at this critical moment.
(Signed) D. Haig F.M.
Commander-in-Chief
British Armies in France
General Headquarters
Tuesday, April 11th, 1918

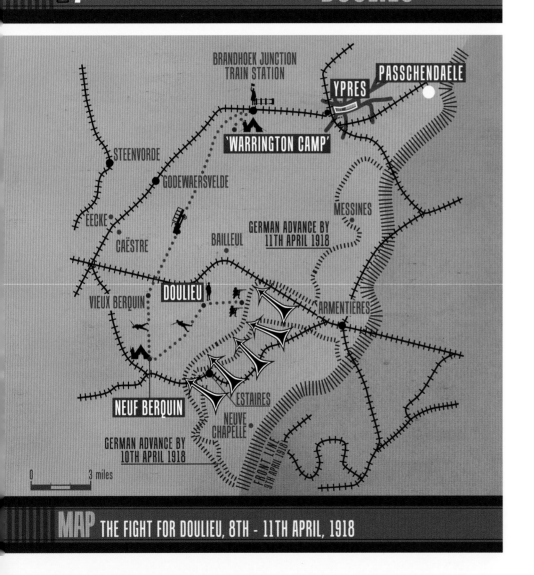

Map labels: BRANDHOEK JUNCTION TRAIN STATION · YPRES · PASSCHENDAELE · 'WARRINGTON CAMP' · STEENVORDE · GODEWAERSVELDE · EECKE · CAËSTRE · BAILLEUL · MESSINES · GERMAN ADVANCE BY 11TH APRIL 1918 · DOULIEU · VIEUX BERQUIN · ARMENTIÈRES · NEUF BERQUIN · ESTAIRES · NEUVE CHAPELLE · GERMAN ADVANCE BY 10TH APRIL 1918 · FRONT LINE 9TH APRIL 1918 · 0 3 miles

MAP THE FIGHT FOR DOULIEU, 8TH - 11TH APRIL, 1918

THE REGIMENT
DECIMATED

As the RGLI moved forward they came under heavy machine gun fire and by that afternoon B and C companies had been decimated. A and D Companies together with men from Battalion Headquarters managed to hold their section of the line for a little longer before withdrawing to a position to the East of Doulieu. The Germans bypassed this area, but the RGLI were soon on the move again with the Battalion Diary for the 12th of April noting that: "At 1.30 A.M. the Battalion took up a new position 3,000 yds (about 2.7km) SW of Doulieu being forced to withdraw." They held on there for a few hours before being out-flanked and withdrawing and digging in yet again. Each withdrawal meant the loss of more men and the casualty lists show how much the Battalion suffered. By the evening of the 12th of April losses were so heavy that the Battalion was down to the equivalent of a single Company. On the 13th of April this much depleted force faced more heavy attacks, and was forced to withdraw further to Bleu Farm. Here they again came under heavy artillery fire, and withdrew even further to a railway cutting on the Hazebrouck to Bailleul line. The line was stabilised here and the few remaining men of the RGLI held on until they were relieved during the night of the 13/14th of April by men of the Australian Army. They then proceeded into billets between Caëstre and St Sylvestre-Cappel, not far from Bailleul. Casualty lists for the 13th of April show a total of over 150 men missing in action, as well as large numbers of men wounded or killed. Many of the bodies were never found, and these men are commemorated on the Ploegsteert memorial a few miles south of Ieper (Ypres) in Belgium. This memorial carries the names of 101 Guernseymen, 94 of them Royal Guernsey Light Infantry men. Private Le Poidevin was lucky in that he was part of the 10% held in reserve. When the order came to move he was delayed by travel problems so that by the time he reached the front, the fighting days of the RGLI were over.

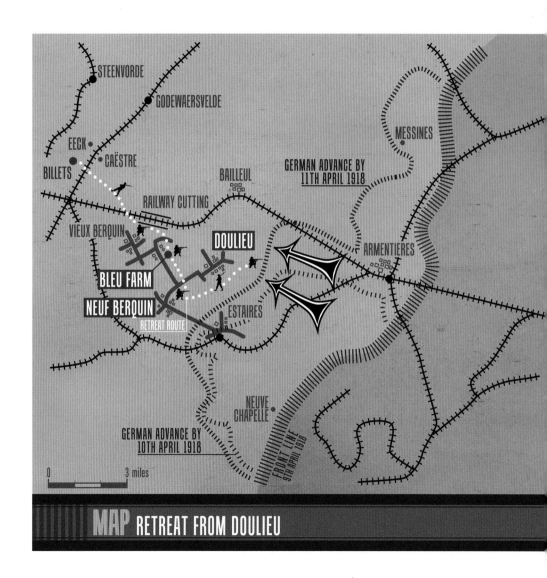

MAP RETREAT FROM DOULIEU

DOULIEU

1918 14TH APRIL

"we got something to eat in a hospital that the British had left, and a good wash up."

"So in the morning we joined the remainder of the Battalion, which was 55 men and two Officers. In this push the Battalion lost 474 men and N.C.O.s and 17 Officers. This is where we lost our Company Commander Captain H.E.K. Stranger who had been rewarded with the M.C. We also lost our platoon commander, Lieutenant J. Stranger. This Officer has joined us while we were at Ypres. This Captain Stranger M.C. was the second son of Mr William Stranger of St Sampson's. He was the first Officer of the First RGLI to receive a military distinction, and a month after we heard that he had died of wounds in a hospital abroad, on May 11th 1918. Lieutenant J. Stranger, who was his brother, was taken prisoner of war in April 1918, and died soon after.

After we had joined the Battalion, we got something to eat in a hospital that the British had left, and a good wash up. Then we marched passed this village Caëstre, and got billeted in a farm. From this place we made trenches in reserve. By the time we left this place the shells was falling very thick, and by us being so very few men in the Battalion they could only make two companies, and the same with the Lancashires that was in the same Brigade, so between the both of us we made a Battalion."

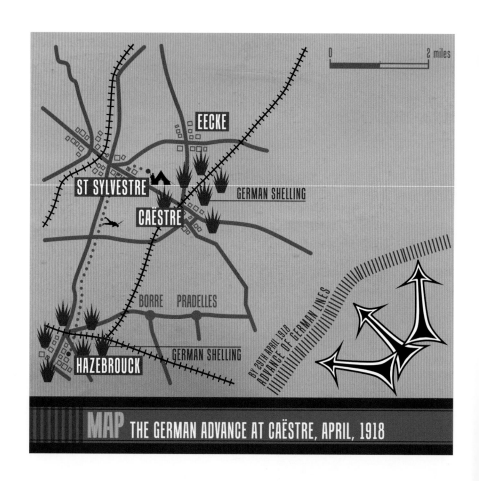

MAP THE GERMAN ADVANCE AT CAËSTRE, APRIL, 1918

> " We left on April 19th 1918, and marched towards Hazebrouck. From this place we did the same work as before, only more on the right of Caëstre, every day passing Hazebrouck which the Germans shelled day after day. At the side of this Farm where we were billeted there was a light railway which was called Hecke-Meulon. We were kept at this place for over a week, so one morning we was told to clean up our gear as the Brigade commander was going to inspect us during the afternoon and was going to give us a speech. We all wondered what was going to happen, we all thought it was for the line again. Well to our surprise this afternoon which was on the 27th of April 1918, the speech was to tell us that the Battalion was relieving us the same day, and to wish us au revoir and farewell. He had been very pleased to have the Guernsey Battalion in his Brigade, and he thanked us for the good work we had done while under his command. He wished us all good luck and of course we returned the same. So we left the 86 Brigade which belong to the 29th Division on the 27th of April 1918.
>
> We came away the same day from Hazebrouck having the 29 Division brass band to lead us down to the station. On our way down we passed some of the Battalions of the 29th going for the line. We arrived at a station called Ebblinghem and camped for the night in a few tents which we put up for the night. The next morning we packed them up again and marched for the station. We left this station on the 28th of April and as the train was leaving the brass band of the Division played the farewell. On our way we passed St-Omer, also the quarries in which some of the Guernsey boys was working. During the night we arrived at Etaples and from the Station marched to No. 9 rest camp. "

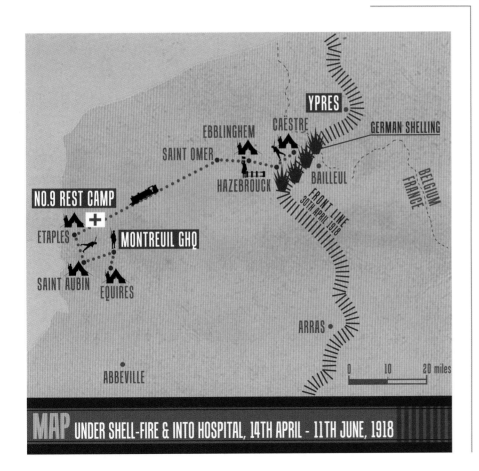

MAP UNDER SHELL-FIRE & INTO HOSPITAL, 14TH APRIL - 11TH JUNE, 1918

1918 29TH APRIL

> *We left this camp on the 29th April and our little band in front marched through the town of Etaples and got billeted in a village called St-Aubin. I was only a day at this when I was taken sick with trench fever, and was admitted to Hospital on the 1st of May 1918, to No. 24 General Hospital, Etaples. The Battalion left St Aubin on the 3rd of May for Montreuil where they joined the General Headquarters, and kept on GHQ for a time. The Battalion was billeted in a village called Ecuires."*

Men of the 1st (Service) Battalion RGLI on guard at the British GHQ in Montreuil. May 1918.

© Guernsey Museum.

Each issue of Orders will be issued consecutively throughout the year. A fresh series to be commenced with the first issue in each year.

Army Form O. 1810
All Arms.

Unit_____

DAILY ORDERS. PART II. No._____

Date___ 25 ___

N.B.—The Sub. No. of Order and Subject are to be shown in cols. 1 and 2, thus:— 1.—Courts Martial.

Station_____ 24/4/18.

3rd Echelon.

Regimental No., Rank and Name.	Sqdn., Batty. or Co.	Particulars of Casualties, etc., and Date.
1. STRENGTH.		
2219 Sgt Le Huray,	✓	Killed in Action 5/4/18.
152 " Ferbrache,	✓	Died of Wounds 13/4/18.
1105 Pte Marquis,	✓	" " 13/4/18.
1345 Sgt Le Lacheur,	✓	Invalided to England, (W) 8/4/18.
1508 Pte Laine,	✓	" " " " 11/4/18.
1931 " Hayter,	✓	" " " " 11/4/18.
2864 L/C Digard,	✓/M	" " " " 14/4/18.
1858 Pte Seager,	✓	" " " " 14/4/18.
1776 " Poppy,	✓	" " " " 14/4/18.
1165 " Le Noury,	✓	" " " " 14/4/18.
810 " Dorey,	✓	" " " " 14/4/18.
9539 " Goudge,	✓	" " " " 15/4/18.
2528 Cpl Bourel,	✓	" " " " 15/4/18.
2017 Pte Le Tissier,	✓	" " " " 15/4/18.
1818 " Hayes,	✓	" " " " 15/4/18.
1703 " Sheppard,	✓	" " " " 15/4/18.
1580 " Le Page,	✓	" " " " 15/4/18.
1915 Cpl Graham,	✓	" " " " 15/4/18.
1185 Pte Fogarty,	✓	" " " " 15/4/18.
574 " Osborne,	✓	" " " " 15/4/18.
850 " Robilliard,	✓	" " " " 15/4/18.
263 " Tippett,	✓	" " " " 15/4/18.
196 " Queripel,	✓	" " " " 15/4/18.
1652 " Le Cheminant,	✓	" " " " 15/4/18.
1464 " Duquemin,	✓	(S) 7/4/18.
857 L/C Woodward,	✓	" 7/4/18.
749 Pte Le Page,	✓	" 8/4/18.
129 " Jehan,	✓	" 8/4/18.
761 L/C May,	✓	" 10/4/18.
741 Pte Phillips,	✓	" 11/4/18.
1646 L/C Duchemin,	✓	" 11/4/18.
1561 Pte Le Huray,	✓	" 13/4/18.
1855 " Wilkinson,	✓/M	" 13/4/18.
1095 L/C Budge,	✓	" 13/4/18.
404 Pte Carre,	✓	" 13/4/18.
589 " Frampton,	✓/M	" 13/4/18.
1970 " Parris,	✓/M	" 13/4/18.
1979 " Stephens,	✓/M	" 13/4/18.
1805 " Crabb,	✓	" 14/4/18.
1776 L/C Ruffles,	✓	" 14/4/18.
1867 Pte Hawkins,	✓	" 15/4/18.
2/Lieut Clark, A.J.de L.)		From 2nd (R) Bn:
2/Lieut Lucas, E.C.)		Embarked 6/4/18. Disembarked 8/4/18.
2. TRANSFERS.		
To Labour Corps.		
157 Pte Richard, J.	✓	7/4/18. New No. 451355.
746 " Duquemin, H.	✓	28/3/18. " " 515338.
907 " Goddard, C.	✓	28/3/18. " " 515555.
175 " Amond, E.	✓	9/4/18. " " 515819.
1478 " Collenette, F.	✓	9/4/18. " " 515818.
Authy: A.G., O.R. C/435 d/- 23/3/17.		
37 Pte Hall	✓	515819.
Authy: A.G. 655 (M) d/- 5/2/18.		

(6359) Wt.W1241/P226 7,488,000 11/17
McA & W Ltd (E 2124) Forms/1810/25

Officer Commanding or Adjutant.

For Officer I/C Infantry Section No. 1

An extract from the Daily Orders Part II showing the RGLI casualty lists for April 1918.
GMAG 1976.490

Losses sustained in April 1918 on top of those at Cambrai only four months earlier were such that the RGLI was no longer a viable fighting force. Battalion Casualty Lists from the 11th to the 13th of April include the names of almost 400 men wounded, taken prisoner of war, missing or killed in action. The War Diary confirms Private Le Poidevin's report that from the 14th to the 19th of April 1918 the remaining RGLI men were formed into a provisional battalion with the 1st Lancashire Fusiliers, who had also suffered heavy losses. They were billeted between Caëstre and St Silvestre-Cappel at this time, still in the Bailleul region of Northern France and were employed on working parties. This provisional Battalion then moved to Hondeghem where it continued to be employed on working parties until the 27th of April. As they were still close to the line, they still suffered occasional losses. CWGC records show that two RGLI men were killed in action and another nine died of wounds during this period.

SPECIAL
ORDERS

On the 24th of April a Special Order of the Day was issued by Major General Cayley, Commander of the 29th Division. In it he said:

> In bidding Goodbye to the ROYAL GUERNSEY LIGHT INFANTRY on their departure from the 29th Division, I wish to place on record my great regret at their withdrawal. During the 6 months the Regiment has been with the Division, they have constantly displayed high qualities of courage and resolution. Both at CAMBRAI and in the recent fighting around HAZEBROUCK, nothing could have been finer than their conduct. Their record, though short, is one on which they and their fellow islanders can look back upon with the greatest pride.
> I wish Lieut. Col. De HAVILLAND and all RANKS all good fortune in the future.
> D. E. Cayley.
> Major-General.

This is where we used to Mount Guards in mornings

The Battalion War Diary reports that they were relieved in 86th Brigade on the 27th of April 1918 by the Dublin Fusiliers, because of "casualties not being replaced". This stark statement is all that was said officially about the tragic losses that finished the Battalion as a fighting force. On the same day the remnants of the RGLI moved to Ebblinghem, between St Omer and Hazebrouck and away from the main battle lines. On the 29th of April they went by train to Etaples, a huge complex of hospitals and camps near the Channel coast, where they went into rest camp for a night. They then moved again on the 29th of April and went into billets at St Aubin, near the Canche estuary. On the 30th of April the survivors of the battalion were attached to troops guarding Haig's General Headquarters at Montreuil a few miles away.

They remained at St Aubin until the 10th of May 1918 when they moved to Ecuires (spelt Equires in the Battalion War Diary) and took over Guard and Duties at GHQ. General Headquarters was the link between the British Expeditionary Force and the British Government, i.e. between the Commander in Chief of the Army and the Secretary of State for War. It also provided links between the other Allied troops and the British Army. Other functions included managing the transport, medical and veterinary systems, and arranging for supplies to get to the troops.

ADMITTED TO
HOSPITAL

At the same time as the remnants of the Battalion were taking over their duties at GHQ, Private Le Poidevin was admitted to hospital in Etaples suffering from Trench Fever, a common disease of the period. It was transmitted by the bites of body lice which were ever present in the trenches. The chief symptoms were headaches, skin rashes, inflamed eyes and leg pains. Despite such wide-ranging symptoms, which were similar to those of typhoid and influenza, the condition was not particularly serious. However it usually meant spending several weeks in hospital as victims tended to suffer relapses often after intervals of several days. Private Le Poidevin was sent to No. 24 General Hospital in Etaples, which had been established in June 1915 and was to remain until well after the Armistice. The writer Vera Brittain worked here as a Voluntary Aid Detachment (VAD) nurse from the autumn of 1917 to Spring 1918.

Private Le Poidevin describes his experiences as follows:

" *There was over nine months I hadn't laid on a bed"*

1918 MAY

" *When I was taken to hospital I was fetched in a motor ambulance. When I arrived at the hospital I was in the waiting room, then I was taken to No.9 ward. We were about 40 sick in this ward and looked after by three nurses, two day time and one night time. I found my bed quite nice, and it was quite different laying between white sheets. There was over nine months I hadn't laid on a bed. Night and day there was sick getting brought in and taken away. Those going were either taken to another hospital or for Blighty.[31] After a while I was there everything was getting on fine, getting well fed, then when I got a lot better and started to walk about. I used to visit the different hospitals about Etaples as every hospital was close to each other. Then as I got strong enough to work, one of the nurses asked me if I wanted a job as orderly. I was only too pleased to take a job like this. My job was to take the meals around to the sick and wash up. Every morning I had to take in the dirty clothes and bring back clean. One day a French soldier was brought in, so when the doctor came around to visit the sick, I was the only one that could speak to this French man, so I had to speak for the doctor."*

Female drivers of the Voluntary Aid
Detachment with their ambulances.
Etaples, 27th June 1917.

Before war broke out the town of Etaples was noted chiefly
for its small fishing and commercial port and was also
a magnet for artists. The pre-war population amounted
to a little over 5,000, but during the First World War the
town became a vast Allied military camp and then a huge
hospital complex, with many hospitals being under canvas.
These hospitals, which included eleven general, one
stationary, four Red Cross hospitals and a convalescent
depot, could deal with 22,000 wounded or sick. Thus it is
hardly surprising that Private Le Poidevin noted that "every
hospital was close to each other." Once he was up and about
he was employed as an orderly doing routine non-medical
tasks to help the nurses. The fact that he spoke Guernsey
French as well as English at home came in very useful in
dealing with French casualties in an English run hospital.

He states that he travelled there by motor ambulance, which
would have been quite a novelty. Motorised ambulances
to transport the wounded were first used in the Great War.
Initially horse drawn vehicles were used to transport the
wounded from the battlefields but on the 12th of September
1914 a meeting was held at the Royal Automobile Club where
a few members offered to place themselves and their

cars at the disposal of the British Red Cross. The appeal
published in *The Times* of 2 October 1914, was instrumental
in raising funds for the provision of ambulances. The
Salvation Army was a major contributor to this appeal and
within three weeks the Red Cross had sufficient funds to
purchase 512 ambulances. They bought practically every
chassis in the country that was suitable for the purpose.
There were additional appeals, the Dennis-Bayley Fund
and Transport of Wounded Fund which helped maintain the
upkeep of the vehicles and there were also a number of cars
presented as gifts to the Red Cross including at least two
from Guernsey. By the end of the war the Motor Ambulance
Department established by the Red Cross consisted of some
3,446 motor vehicles, including 2,171 motor ambulances
based at strategic points.

HOSPITAL LIFE-
ETAPLES AND TROUVILLE

Private Le Poidevin goes on to describe his hospital experiences, saying that:

1918 19TH MAY

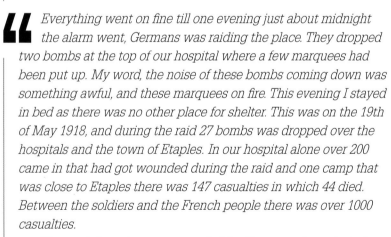

" *Everything went on fine till one evening just about midnight the alarm went, Germans was raiding the place. They dropped two bombs at the top of our hospital where a few marquees had been put up. My word, the noise of these bombs coming down was something awful, and these marquees on fire. This evening I stayed in bed as there was no other place for shelter. This was on the 19th of May 1918, and during the raid 27 bombs was dropped over the hospitals and the town of Etaples. In our hospital alone over 200 came in that had got wounded during the raid and one camp that was close to Etaples there was 147 casualties in which 44 died. Between the soldiers and the French people there was over 1000 casualties.*

The next day when we saw what had happened we started making trenches along side of every ward. The next night was as bad, I thought my last minute had come. About the hospitals was nothing else but dead lying about. But the third night was the worst night for us. When the alarm was given the bombs was already

dropping in the Hospital and before we had time to get in our trenches one bomb fell on No.17 ward, smashing all the windows of our ward. Some couldn't move from their beds, so we used to put the clothes of the ones that was able to walk on those that couldn't move. After the bomb had hit No.17 there was not a piece of ward standing and some of the chaps that was in were never found again. A Canadian Hospital had five Canadian nuns killed, and one of the wards they found a door down with a chap laying on top dead and a nurse in under living. Then after the third night they began clearing the hospital, and only the ones that could walk about was kept back. Then at night time every nurse was carried away in motor ambulances, and we would sleep in the wood for the night, we used to take two or three blankets each and go down by the river for the night. We used to find ourselves back about six o'clock the next morning. This carried on for a week or so, and this week Gerry never came over at all, then he started again on his raiding."

The town's medical prominence had not escaped the attention of the
German military high command, which organised the air raids on the town.
Four such attacks using incendiary bombs were directed against hospital
sites in May 1918. The War Diary of the 7th Canadian Stationary Hospital
confirms Private Le Poidevin's account of events, describing how on the
19th of May 1918, German aeroplanes attacked the hospitals at Etaples. The
entry for Monday the 20th of May states, "Last night, about 10:30 we had a
disastrous air raid as a result of which we lost two men (one killed and the
other died of wounds) and had one man wounded and also the
O. C. Major E. V. Hogan, wounded. Enemy aircraft suddenly were heard, and
began dropping bombs without our having received warning. Practically
the entire Etaples hospital area was subjected to an aerial bombardment for
fully an hour, after which the raiders departed, returning again some time
after midnight, and dropped more bombs. They also employed machine
guns. It is unofficially estimated that the total casualties in the Etaples area
were about one thousand. Casualties were numerous in the staffs of several
of the hospitals, and certain patients were also casualties."

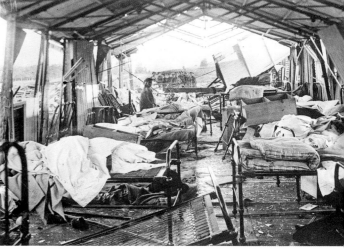

"

*I thought my last minute
had come"*

BOMBED
HOSPITAL

The war diary of Miss Maud McCarthy, the Matron-in-Chief to the British Expeditionary Force[32] confirms Private Le Poidevin's account of digging trenches and going out into the countryside, stating that "...Everywhere strong dug-outs are being made and in the meantime the whole of the day staff are being taken into the country in details with 2 officers and 2 NCOs in charge, the Matron and night staff remaining with the hospital." The "Summary of Inspections and Work done during the month away from Headquarters" for the 31st of May 1918 describes how "...There was a terrible raid right over the hospitals. Practically all the Etaples hospitals suffered, those which had the most casualties being the St John's Ambulance Brigade hospital, where 1 Sister was killed and 5 wounded, besides many patients and personnel, the Liverpool Merchant's Hospital (1 Sister wounded), No.24 General Hospital[33] (2 of the nursing staff wounded, one severely), No.56 General Hospital, where there were no casualties amongst the nursing staff but the administrative block was almost destroyed, and No.26 General Hospital, as well as the two Canadian hospitals (Nos.1 and 7) which had suffered so severely before. The St. John's Ambulance Brigade Hospital, which was beautifully equipped, is entirely wrecked."

Miss McCarthy's account continues on the 1st of June: "Etaples air-raid: Received telephone message from Etaples saying that there had been a very bad air-raid the night before – nearly all the hospitals in the Etaples area had suffered, particularly the St. John's Ambulance Brigade Hospital, Liverpool Merchant's Hospital, 24,[34] 26 and 56 General Hospitals. At the SJAB Hospital one Sister had been killed and 5 wounded and a few others were suffering from shock. At No.24 General Hospital, Miss Freshfield, VAD, had been seriously wounded in the head, and one other Sister had been slightly wounded. Informed Matron-in-Chief, War Office, and BRCS, and DGMS." Again all of this tallies closely with Private Le Poidevin's account of what he witnessed.

However his time at Etaples was coming to an end. He writes:

" Somehow or other I happened to pick up some bits of shell which poisoned my blood causing a rash over my body. The day before I left this hospital there was only three or four chaps left in my ward. These were getting the same sort of rash as myself, and on the 6th of June in the afternoon I left this hospital for another. We were fetched in motor buses for the station, then we got on a British Red Cross train. We had 18 hours journey, then from a station near Trouville we got on a light railway, which took us right up alongside of our hospital which was No.72 General Hospital, Trouville, J block, No. 4 ward. This was a very nice place, also a very large place. The hospital itself could hold 5,000 men, and there were two other hospitals which were as large. These three hospitals were close to each other, and besides they were 3 Convalescent camps with 5,000 men in each.

After I had been in this hospital for a week, I was marked out fit, then I had to give in my blue suit and get a new suit of khaki. Leaving this hospital on the 11th June I was sent to No.15 Convalescent camp and put in R Company, No. 8 Hut. This was one of the finest places going, there were all kinds of sports every day, and two or three times a week we were marched down to the beach, which was about two miles away, having the brass band to lead us down.

above
Recovering British soldiers from No. 14 Convalescent Depot on a 'Bathing Parade' at the beach, Trouville. August 1918.

Q 11240. © Imperial War Museums.

far left
The remains of a ward destroyed by a German bomb in the St. John's Ambulance Brigade Hospital complex, Etaples. May 1918.

Q 293. © Imperial War Museums.

HOSPITAL LIFE-
ETAPLES AND TROUVILLE

Recovering British soldiers from
No. 14 Convalescent Depot out for a
morning run, Trouville. August 1918.

Q 11239. © Imperial War Museums.

1918 JUNE

" *From this camp we were allowed out in the different villages nearby, only in the town of Trouville we had to have passes. We had to write out all the places and roads that was out of bounds. Here are the names of these places:*

Cafe Blighty bar, Rue de La Mer.
Cafe Venot in Rue Pont L'Eveque,
Cafe Hudieson,   "
Cafe Lion D'or   "
Cafe Lecorna Reverick   "
Hotel Tresnon, Rue Carnot

Private Le Poidevin mentions a rash that he and the other men suffered as a result of having picked up "some bits of shell which poisoned my blood." Recurring rashes were one of the symptoms of Trench Fever, but are not typical of blood poisoning. However allergic reactions to the chemicals in some of the shells

A recovering British soldier wearing his blue 'hospital' uniform. Circa 1914-1918.
© Guernsey Museum.

RECOVERING IN
HOSPITAL

may well also have caused rashes. In any case he seems to have recovered fairly quickly from this. No. 72 General Hospital at Trouville, where he was sent for the next stage of recuperation, was opened in December 1917 and remained there until October 1919. The official diary of the Matron-in-Chief, British Expeditionary Force:[35] described it saying, "There are two hospitals already established and a third unit in the making, all composed of 2500 beds, entirely hutted, with fine accommodation for officers, Nursing Sisters and men. The hospital is built in self-contained blocks of 250 beds, each a little hospital in itself. Each unit has accommodation for 100 officers and the rest is for men. They have most splendid mess, dining rooms, kitchens, store-rooms, a great big reception hut and a good administrative block. The Sisters' quarters are first-rate in every respect

– a great big mess and ante-room and accommodation for 125 people in cubicles, all under cover and connected by corridors. There are 4 bath-rooms only. All the out-houses, kitchens, etc. are first-rate, similar to those in our other units but larger in comparison. The unit is lighted with electricity and heated with coal stoves, and when the road is made and they have got rid of the mud, it will be first-rate. It is situated on the top of a hill. At the time of the visit 72 General Hospital had 1600 patients and they were taking in at 73 General Hospital the next day. They are beginning to lay out the grounds and are going to have large vegetable gardens."

Private Le Poidevin mentions having to give in his blue suit and get a new khaki one. This clearly distinguishable bright blue uniform with a red tie was useful

in helping medical staff to identify their patients but it also marked out those who had 'done their bit' when they were out and about, so that they wouldn't be considered to be 'shirkers'. Once he was no longer a hospital patient he returned to the normal khaki uniform. He also mentions going down to the beach once he was in Convalescent Camp.

CONVALESCENT
DEPOTS

Convalescent or Command Depots were half way houses for casualties returning to the front - men who no longer required hospitalisation but were not yet fit to rejoin their units. Photographs in the collection of the Imperial War Museum[36] show that the Depot at Trouville had its own brass band consisting of convalescent bandsmen from various units and as Private Le Poidevin stated, it led groups of convalescents to the beach for their daily exercise. There were also open air concerts, boxing matches and other forms of entertainment put on by and for the convalescent troops. The places that were out of bounds are all cafés except one which is a hotel. Alcohol and/ or women might be found in such places and therefore provide sources of trouble for the convalescent soldiers. Some establishments were also deemed to be for 'officers only', not for Other Ranks such as Private Le Poidevin.

Accommodation huts for British
soldiers in No. 14 Convalescent
Depot, Trouville. August 1918.

1918 25TH JUNE

> *I left this convalescent camp on the 25th of June 1918. There were squads leaving this camp every afternoon, for the base. From this camp we marched to a station in Trouville, being a few hundred together. Here we got on a Red Cross train which was very cosy. We arrived at Rouen at about midnight, where we had something to eat and a bed till the morning, and about 10 o'clock the next morning we marched off for our base. I stayed at the base for about a week, and then I was sent off for the Battalion. From the Base we marched for the station, we were four Guernseys together, and got up in the old cattle truck. From Rouen we passed Abbeville and stopped at Etaples and took another train for Montreuil, then from the Station we marched through the town of Montreuil where we found here and there some of our Battalion on duty. Then at last we got to the Battalion headquarters, I got put in the same company, C, this being on the 3rd of July.*

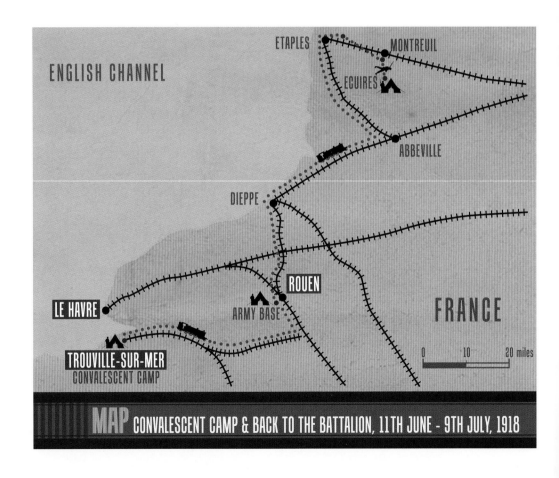

MAP CONVALESCENT CAMP & BACK TO THE BATTALION, 11TH JUNE - 9TH JULY, 1918

Two soldiers of the 1st (Service) Battalion RGLI on sentry duty outside the main gates to the chateau. Circa June - October 1918.
© Guernsey Museum.

1918 4TH JULY

" *The next day I was sent on fatigue down to the station. The job I had was on loading trucks and while I was on this job trains was passing. One train stopped and I could hear chaps calling me. I found this funny that these chaps knew me, so I went over to speak to them, and I found out that it was the Guernsey Royal Engineers, they were changing fronts. I went on different jobs for three or four days, then on the 9th July 1918 I left Ecuires, and was sent up to the château where the Commander of the British Army stayed. I was on anti-aircraft there. The place was called Le Château, an out of the way place. The nearest village was about two miles, which was Ecuires or Brimeux. The town was about the same distance. On this job we were about 20 of us and had a day on duty and a day off.*"

FRANCE

ETAPLES

RANG-DU-FLIERS

BERCK

MONTREUIL

ECUIRES

WAILLY BEAUCAMP

CHÂTEAU DE BEAUREPAIRE
HAIG'S RESIDENCE AT SAINT NICHOLAS

0   2 miles

MAP ANTI-AIRCRAFT DUTY AT HAIG'S RESIDENCE, 9TH JULY - 7TH AUGUST, 1918

GUARD
DUTIES

Private Le Poidevin's time as a convalescent soon came to an end and he was ready to rejoin his unit. The "Guernsey Royal Engineers" mentioned here would have been 245 (Guernsey) Army Troops Company, Royal Engineers. This unit was formed in 1918 from soldiers of the Royal Engineers Company formed when the Militia was disbanded, plus some men from the Alderney Militia and a few transferred from the RGLI. The Engineers left Guernsey in March of that year and remained in France until July 1918. They were employed in tasks such as strengthening defence lines, building pontoon bridges over the river Marne, and finally rebuilding rest camps. In July they were transferred to Belgium and given the job of improving the front and support lines in the Ypres sector. This explains why they were on the train passing through Montreuil when Private Le Poidevin was working there.

The Battalion War Diary reports that the remnants of the RGLI remained at Ecuires (or Equires) furnishing Guards and Duties for GHQ from June to the end of October 1918. Divided into five departments, the General Headquarters based at Montreuil was an enormous administrative body staffed with a wide range of military personnel, from private soldiers to field officers, with at its head Field Marshal Sir Douglas Haig, Commander-in-Chief of the British Army. Ecuires is a suburb of Montreuil-sur-Mer which was chosen as the base for General Headquarters from 1916 onwards. Its geographical position was ideal because many British bases on French soil (ports, garrisons, training camps, depots etc.) were within easy reach. It was situated far enough from the front line, which was fairly static by this time, to be relatively safe but close enough to allow easy communications. It was also roughly halfway between the Allied capitals of London and Paris. Montreuil also had the capacity to house the various departments of GHQ within the numerous buildings of its enormous former military academy. Sir Douglas Haig, Commander in Chief of the British Army, was based at Beaurepaire, an isolated chateau about 20 miles (approximately 32 km.) from GHQ.

Field Marshall Sir Douglas Haig's Headquarters at the Château de Beaurepaire, St. Nicolas (near Montreuil).

far left
Men of the 1st (Service) Battalion RGLI mounting guard outside the main gates to the chateau. Circa June – October 1918.
© Guernsey Museum.

top left
Men of the RGLI Signal Section posing for a group photograph outside the armoured walls around the chateau. Circa June – October 1918.
© Guernsey Museum.

above
Men of the RGLI Band posing for a group photograph outside the armoured walls around the chateau. Circa June – October 1918.
© Guernsey Museum.

" Here we spent a very happy time"

1918 7TH AUGUST

Private Le Poidevin describes the work he did there:

" On the 7th of August we left this place with the advance General Headquarters, being carried in motor lorries. This is the names of some of the villages we passed on our way, the first being, Wailly, then Nemport, Vron, Liercourt, Abbeville, Airaines, and Allery. The next place we stayed at, Wiry-Au-Mont, we put up two tents in a wood near this station where the commander had his train. Our work was on anti-aircraft over this train. Here we spent a very happy time. I visited a few villages which was around this place, such as Hallencourt, which was 5 Kilometres away, Allery, and Merélessart. We had a little more work at this place, we had a day on and the next day on fatigue whether on the train or to the Quartermaster's stores. One day while I was down at the Quartermaster's Stores I was sent with the driver on a motor lorry to fetch a load of petroleum. On our way we passed these villages: Allery, Airaines, then to Pont Rémy which was 20 Kilometres. Then as there was none there, we were sent to another station, passing Le Catelet, Conde-Folie, Longpré [37] and Doullens, to Fant-Freres [38] station, where we loaded up. Coming back we passed Flexicourt, Vignacourt, Airaines, Allery and back to Wiry au Mont. Every day one of us was sent to Montreuil for mail for the Staff, being 90 miles from the Battalion".

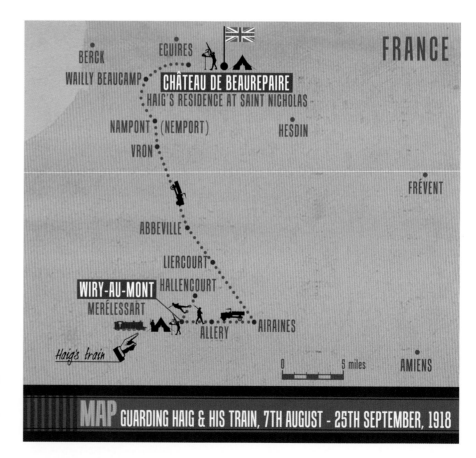

MAP GUARDING HAIG & HIS TRAIN, 7TH AUGUST - 25TH SEPTEMBER, 1918

Men of the 1st (Service) Battalion RGLI providing a Guard of Honour for (from Left) Field Marshall Sir Douglas Haig (Commander-in-Chief of the British Expeditionary Force), Maréchal Ferdinand Foch (Commander-in-Chief of the Allied Armies, March 1918), Captain E.H.P. Hutchinson(?), RGLI, French President Raymond Poincaré and His Majesty King George V.
GMAG 6591B. © Guernsey Museum.

After his time in hospital Private Le Poidevin appears to have resumed his duties as a Lewis gunner and was placed on anti-aircraft duties first guarding the chateau which Sir Douglas Haig was using as his base, then at Haig's mobile Advanced H.Q. The RGLI War Diary reported that at midday on the 7th of August 1918 a hundred men and three officers from the Battalion formed the Guard of Honour for H.M. the King, Field Marshal Sir Douglas Haig, Maréchal Foch, Généralissimé of the Allied Armies and the French President Poincaré at the chateau.

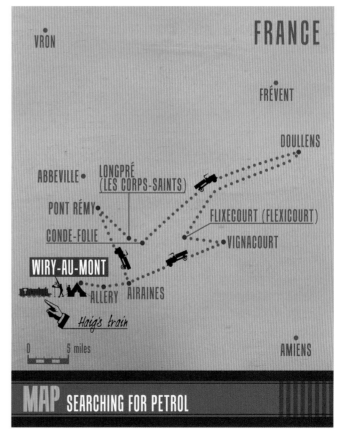

FRANCE

VRON

FRÉVENT

DOULLENS

ABBEVILLE • LONGPRÉ
(LES CORPS-SAINTS)

PONT RÉMY •

FLIXECOURT (FLEXICOURT)

CONDE-FOLIE

VIGNACOURT

WIRY-AU-MONT

ALLERY   AIRAINES

Haig's train

0   5 miles

AMIENS

MAP SEARCHING FOR PETROL

GHQ AND ADVANCED HQ

GUARDING
HAIG

This was also the day on which Private Le Poidevin's group left in motor lorries for Advanced H.Q, but no mention is made of this in the War Diary. Sir Douglas Haig however wrote in his personal diary that his Advanced Headquarters was established in his special train at Wiry–au-Mont Station on that same day.[39] This mobile headquarters allowed him to travel to meet with other leaders in areas close to the Front. Wiry-au-Mont is in Picardie, some 10 miles (12 km) from both Abbeville and Amiens and with good rail connections to both, and is about 50 miles (80km) from Montreuil-sur-Mer. On the 8th of August, the day after Private Le Poidevin started his tour of duty guarding Haig's train, the Allies launched the Hundred Days offensive, starting with the battle of Amiens.

The Battalion Diary also notes that on 14th August 2nd Lieutenant N. Ingrouille, Platoon Commander, was presented with the Royal Victorian Order, 5th Class by H.M. the King at Tramecourt, for commanding guard at his chateau. The King had taken up temporary residence at Tramecourt so that he could visit the troops with the aim of raising morale. Private Le Poidevin doesn't mention this, presumably because he was away from Montreuil with Advance H.Q. at the time. However he does mention travelling by motor lorry in search of petrol when he was on fatigue for the Quartermaster's

stores. Sir Travers Clarke, Quartermaster General at GHQ, had built up a Motor Lorry Reserve which would be available for transporting goods if ever the railway system was unable to be used for that purpose.[40] There was a real fear at this time that the Germans would break through the railway network and cause major logistical problems for the British Army. He was also aware that if, in the worst case scenario, a retreat to the coastal ports was needed, alternative transport would be required. Presumably the petrol was needed for this reserve. The villages mentioned here cover a triangle between Wiry, Amiens and Doullens, so they covered quite a wide area in their search for fuel.

The Battalion War Diaries make no mention of men being based at Boubers or the other towns and villages mentioned by Private Le Poidevin. It states that for the period 01.08.1918 to 31.08.1918, the Battalion was billeted at Ecuires (or Equires) while it furnished guards and duties for GHQ. Boubers-sur-Canche is a small village which was an airship base for the Royal Flying Corps for part of the war. It is very close to Frévent, which Private Le Poidevin also mentions. Because of its position, Frévent was a place of some importance on the lines of communication. Part of the Lucknow Casualty Clearing

MAP GUARDING HAIG & HIS TRAIN, 25TH SEPTEMBER - 5TH OCTOBER, 1918

Map labels: BERCK, MONTREUIL, ECUIRES, BRIMEUX, LESPINOY, MARESQUET / ECQUIMECOURT, BOUIN-PLUMOISON, MARCONNELLE, HESDIN, WAIL, GALAMETZ, AUBROMETZ, BOUBERS, LIGNY, FRÉVENT, HAUTEVILLE, FOSSEUX, AVESNES, LIENCOURT, BAVINCOURT, GOUY EN ARTOIS, ABBEVILLE, DOULLENS, *Haig's train*, WIRY-AU-MONT, AMIENS, 0 5 miles

Station, the 6th Stationary Hospital, the 3rd Canadian Casualty Clearing Station and the 19th and 43rd Casualty Clearing Stations were based there during the war years. Hesdin was the H.Q .of General Byng, Commander of the British Third Army at this stage of the war, and all of these villages are along the main road out of Hesdin to the East towards Arras. The Château St Nicolas which Private Le Poidevin mentions is probably Beaurepaire, Haig's GHQ, as it is actually 4 kms (just over 2 miles) south east of Montreuil on the D138, at St Nicolas.

1918 25TH SEPTEMBER

" *After a while at this place we started on another turn with the Advanced General Headquarters, leaving this place on the 25th of September. We were carried in motor lorries passing these villages: Brimeux, Lespinoy, Maresquet, Ecquimecourt, Bouin-Plumoisin, Marconnelle, Hesdin, Vaile, St. Georges, Galametz, Aubrometz, Boubers, Ligny, Frévent, Rebreuviette, Liencourt, Avesnes, Hauteville, Fosseux and stayed at Gouy-en-Artois. We put up our tents in under a few apple trees. We were lucky as they were loaded with fruit. I visited a village called Bavincourt. We had a nice time here, and one afternoon a motor lorry loaded with chaps from the Battalion came to relieve the ones that was for leave. I was one of the lucky ones and left at about 6 o'clock in the afternoon on the 5th October, 1918 arriving at the Battalion about midnight. The Battalion was still at Ecuires, only billeted in huts. But the next day, instead of going on leave I was sent on fatigue down to the station, and the following day on guard. This carried on till the 29th of October 1918, when I left the Battalion for leave.*"

GHQ AND ADVANCED HQ

THE END
IN SIGHT

On the 15th of August, Marshal Ferdinand Foch had demanded that General Haig continue the Amiens offensive even though the attack was faltering as the troops outran their supplies and artillery. Also German reserves were being moved to the sector. Foch had been given overall control to co-ordinate the activities of the Allied Armies on the 26th of March 1918 at the Doullens Conference, and at a later conference he was given the title Supreme Commander of the Allied Armies with the title of Généralissimé (Supreme General). Haig instead prepared to launch a fresh offensive at Albert, on the Somme, which opened on the 21st of August. Albert was captured the next day then on the 26th of August the Second Battle of Arras began. The Amiens and Arras offensives were both successful for the Allies, but resulted in very heavy losses for the Germans, who were forced to retreat behind the Hindenburg line. Foch and Haig then worked together to plan the Grand Offensive, which started on the 26th of September 1918 and had the aim of breaking the Hindenburg line.

Private Le Poidevin notes that they moved to Gouy-en-Artois, a small village about 14km (9 miles) south of Arras on the day before the opening of the battle, again indicating that he was with Haig's Advance Headquarters. Brimeux, his starting point, is near Montreuil and the other places form a line between there and the outskirts of Arras. Bavincourt is also close to Arras and a rest camp was based there at this time. This camp is described as being "charmingly situated"[41], run on model lines and with excellent entertainment and sports days for the troops. On the 5th of October Private Le Poidevin's planned leave appears to have been cancelled and he returned to GHQ. The cancellation may have been related to the fact that the 5th of October 1918 was the date on which the German government resigned, realizing that defeat was inevitable. On the 6th of October newspapers reported that Austria, Germany and Turkey were asking for an Armistice. Private Le Poidevin eventually went on leave on the 29th of October, by which time detailed arrangements for an Armistice were being discussed.

He describes his rather complicated journey back home to Guernsey saying:

"the weather was rough and raining and I partly lost my way."

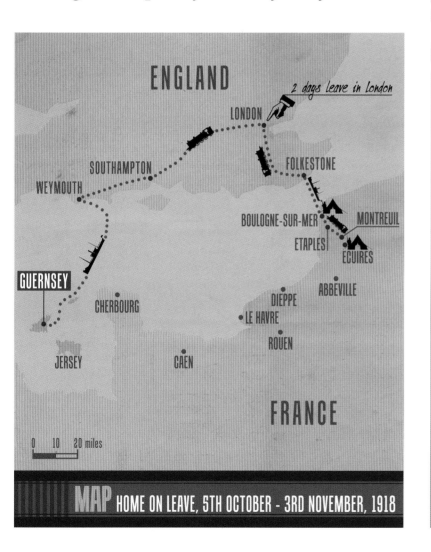

ENGLAND

2 days Leave in London

LONDON

SOUTHAMPTON

FOLKESTONE

WEYMOUTH

BOULOGNE-SUR-MER   MONTREUIL

ETAPLES

ECUIRES

GUERNSEY

ABBEVILLE

CHERBOURG

DIEPPE

LE HAVRE

ROUEN

JERSEY   CAEN

FRANCE

0   10   20 miles

MAP HOME ON LEAVE, 5TH OCTOBER - 3RD NOVEMBER, 1918

1918 NOVEMBER

" We marched down to the station of Montreuil taking the train to Etaples, and another from Etaples to Boulogne, where we stayed in a rest camp for the night. The next morning we got on board ship and arrived at Folkestone, England after two hours journey. Then at Folkestone we took the train for Victoria station, arriving at about 5 o'clock. Then we had to change our French money into English money. Then we inquired at an enquiry office for the train for Southampton and the time the boats was sailing. That evening there were no boats sailing from Southampton, only from Weymouth, but we were too late, the train had left 5 minutes ago. So in coming away from this office I met some of our boys, and we decided to look out for some place to rest for the night, which we did and rested in a Y.M.C.A.

The next morning we went up to Whitehall and had two days extension on our leave, spending these two days about London. Then after our two days we left Waterloo during the afternoon for Southampton, arriving about 2 o'clock. Then the news we had was that all the berths was taken, and they advised us to take the train for Weymouth and catch the boat which was leaving at 1 o'clock in the morning. This I did but when I arrived at Weymouth and went out from the station, the weather was rough and raining and I partly lost my way. It was only with help from a policeman that I found the docks, and got on board, and had a good sleep, waking up in the morning to find that I was still in Weymouth and that the boat was not leaving before the following night on account of rough weather. I spent this day in Weymouth and arrived in Guernsey the following morning on the 3rd of November 1918."

LATIMER
ON LEAVE

The Railway companies ran a regular ferry service to the islands right through the war years, with the Great Western Railway Company operating out of Weymouth and the London and South Western Railway Company boats leaving from Southampton. The boat trains for both ports left from London's Waterloo station. Private Le Poidevin and his colleagues had come into Victoria Station from Folkestone and found they couldn't get home immediately so they found a bed for the night in a Y.M.C.A. hostel. In "The Romance of the Red Triangle"[42], Sir Arthur Keysall Yapp describes how "...Tommy recognises it to-day as his club, his meeting house, his home from home. It is his, and he knows it! It touches him at every point and in almost every place. The recruit finds it at his depôt, near his billet, and in the training camp where he learns to be a soldier; indeed, it is part of the training, and an important part, too. Passing through London or a great provincial city, he can stay the night in one of the Y.M.C.A. hostels; he meets it again at the English ports before he embarks for one of the fighting fronts; it is there to greet him on the other side." Hostels had been established in all these places since the early years of the war and their red triangle sign was familiar to the soldiers so it is not surprising that Private Le Poidevin chose this as his place for an unexpected overnight stay. He noted that on the following day he had to go to Whitehall to get his leave extended because of the delays in travelling. Here he visited the War Office building which in those days housed the Directorates and staff who dealt with recruitment, movement and supply for the troops. Once he was in possession of the correct documentation he was able to have a short break in London before setting off again for Guernsey.

Fortunately there was a direct rail connection between Southampton and Weymouth so that the Guernseymen could move on when they found that there was no room on the Southampton boat. The weather must have been dreadful to delay the boat to such an extent as they had a history of running even in extreme conditions and despite frequent U boat sightings. Several of their captains were awarded the O.B.E. (listed in the final list of war honours in *the London Gazette* [43] for their service during the war years).

A Y.M.C.A. Hostel in Europe, circa 1914-15.
GMAG 1995.121.

1918 11TH NOVEMBER

"" *While I was on leave the Armistice was signed, this being on the 11th November 1918, this giving a much better leave. As I was leaving the Battalion, the orders were that they were leaving the next day from Ecuires for a month's training, which meant for the firing line after. After spending a happy time while on leave, I left Guernsey on the 15th of November 1918, bound for France again. From Guernsey we arrived at Weymouth in the evening, and stayed at Weymouth for the night, taking the train the next morning for Waterloo. The following night we slept in London, and took the train on the 18th November for Folkestone. We spent a few hours in this town before embarking for France.*

We arrived at Boulogne about 6 o'clock in the evening and marched up to St Martin's camp, where we stayed two days before being sent to join our Battalion. We joined the Battalion at Rang-du-Fliers on the 21st of November 1918.

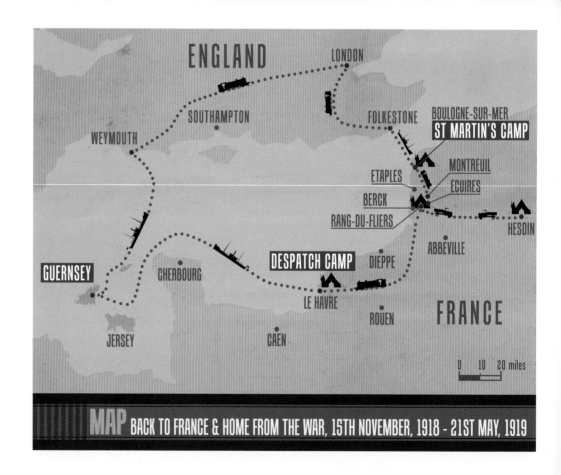

MAP BACK TO FRANCE & HOME FROM THE WAR, 15TH NOVEMBER, 1918 - 21ST MAY, 1919

"While I was on leave the Armistice was signed"

"We spent our Xmas at this place and left Rang-du-Fliers on the 27th December for Hesdin, about 60 men. The remainder of the Battalion went for Montreuil on GHQ. We were carried in motor lorries for Hesdin. This place was about 20 miles from Montreuil. At Hesdin we were billeted in French barracks in the town, a very nice place. While I was there I visited a few villages and so passed my New Year. On 3rd May 1919 a French regiment came, after being away since the war had started. From this place I often when I had a day off visited the boys at Montreuil, taking the train in the morning and arriving back again in the evening."

RETURN TO DUTIES
AND DEMOBILISATION

Photograph of the front cover of Les Folies Magazine. Hand-written by the men of B Company, 1st (Service) Battalion, RGLI during December 1918. The magazine contains sketch-work and prose.
GMAG 1855. © Guernsey Museum.

BACK TO
ECUIRES

Reinforcements 17 and 18 from the 2nd Battalion RGLI based in Guernsey had travelled out during October 1918 to join the 1st Battalion at Ecuires. Reinforcement 17 consisting of 52 men went out on the 15th, but numbers are not listed for reinforcement 18 which travelled on the 29th. These were the last reinforcements of the RGLI to qualify for the British War Medal and Victory Medal. Then on the 31st of October the Battalion, with the exception of A and D companies, moved to Les Folies camp at Rang du Fliers, a small town on the road between Montreuil and Berck-sur-Mer. A and D Companies followed on the 4th of November. Here they started training in order to be ready for a return to the line. However the Armistice was signed on the 11th of November, whilst Private Le Poidevin was on leave, so he never returned to the Front Line. He reports staying overnight at St Martin's camp, which was a rest camp in the hills above Boulogne before moving on to Rang-du-Fliers then on to Hesdin by motor lorry with about 60 colleagues on the 27th of December. This fits with information in the Battalion War Diaries, which notes that all companies continued training at Rang-du-Fliers until the 2nd of January 1919.

The Battalion moved back to
Ecuires in January 1919, where
according to the diary they took
over all duties from 1st Battalion
Honourable Artillery Company,
furnishing Guards and Duties at
GHQ until the end of the month.
On the 24th of January their
Service banner was consecrated
by the Right Reverend Bishop
Gwynne, assisted by the Reverend
H.C.Collings, Chaplain to the
RGLI. It was then presented to
the Battalion by the Chief of the
General Staff Lieutenant General
the Honourable Sir Hubert
Lawrence, K.C.B. on behalf of the
War Office. These Union Flags
were presented to every Service
Battalion at the end of the Great
War and the RGLI banner now
rests in the Town Church in St
Peter Port, Guernsey.

IN FRENCH
BARRACKS

Private Le Poidevin doesn't mention this significant event, but he reports being billeted in French barracks in the town of Hesdin with about 60 men of the RGLI from late December 1918. They remained there until May 1919 when the French regiment which had been based there before the war returned. This was probably the 2nd Battalion of the 73rd Régiment d'Infanterie de Ligne, who were based at the Caserne Tripier in Hesdin until the 5th of August 1914 and returned in 1919. Hesdin was on the main Arras to Montreuil road at that time, though new roads have been built since. In 1916 it had become General Headquarters (2nd Echelon) and was the H.Q. of the 3rd Army. There were several hospitals nearby plus a Royal Air Force base. It was also where the then National War Museum stored early items for its Great War collection, later to become the Imperial War Museum collection.

Private Le Poidevin's last entry notes that:

1919 17TH MAY

"On the 17th of May 1919 during the day the names of men that was going to be demobilised was read out and they had to pack up. The same evening at midnight a motor lorry arrived to fetch us, taking us to Ecuires to join the boys that was getting demobilised from the Battalion. We arrived at two o'clock in the morning. The same morning, after a few hour's sleep we marched from this place to Etaples, which was 15 miles away. At Etaples we took the train for Le Havre arriving at Le Havre at 11 o'clock on the 19th of May 1919. We stayed in a Despatch camp at Le Havre for two days, before sailing for Guernsey, being 9 hours on board before reaching Guernsey. As soon as we landed we marched for Fort George where we got dismissed. After being at Fort George a few days I got demobilised on the 23rd of May 1919. I transferred to Army Reserve on the 23rd of June 1919.

While I was in Active Service in France I wrote and sent 445 letters, and received 458, which made 903 letters altogether. Out of these 445 letters I wrote 189 letters to my wife, and received 238 letters out of 458 from my wife."

The steam ship *Lydia* pulling into the quayside in St. Peter Port Harbour, Guernsey on 22nd May, 1919. Latimer Le Poidevin and the other survivors of the 1st (Service) Battalion RGLI, are aboard. Thomas A Bramley's Real Photo Series (postcard).
GMAG 1975.319. © Guernsey Museum.

This amount of correspondence in wartime might seem surprising, but from the 28th of August 1914 free postage was allowed for postcards and letters weighing less than 4 ounces sent by members of the British Expeditionary Force. A highly efficient postal system operated on the Western Front. All mail bound for the troops there was sorted at the London Home Depot of the Army Postal Service. Covering five acres of Regents Park, this was said to be the largest wooden structure in the world employing over 2,500 mostly female staff by 1918. During the war the Home Depot handled some 2 billion letters and 114 million parcels. In France, the APS established base depots at Le Havre, Boulogne and Calais and mail was carried with munitions on supply trains to the front. In 1917 over 19,000 mailbags crossed the channel each day with half a million bags conveyed in the run up to Christmas. Receiving mail from home was considered to be good for morale and letter writing was encouraged. Rest huts provided by charitable organisations such as the Salvation Army, the Church Army and the YMCA provided postcards and help with letter writing where needed. Unfortunately, according to family sources none of Private Le Poidevin's numerous letters or those of his wife or other relatives survived.

Battalion War Diary entries for the RGLI conclude on the 1st of April 1919, with a final entry saying that they were still at Ecuires furnishing guards and duties for GHQ as they had been since January. Private Le Poidevin notes that he was still at Hesdin on the 3rd of May and visited "the boys at Montreuil" on a regular basis. Exactly what he and the others were doing at Hesdin is unclear but he was still there on the 17th of May when the notice of demobilisation came through. Then they started on the long journey home, via Montreuil to join the others who were being demobilised at the same time. From there they had a fifteen mile (24 km) march to Etaples, then a train ride to Le Havre where they stayed for two days in a rest camp. They embarked for Guernsey on the 21st of May and arrived some 9 hours later on board the S.S. *Lydia*, one of the boats that had kept the regular mailboat service running throughout the war years.

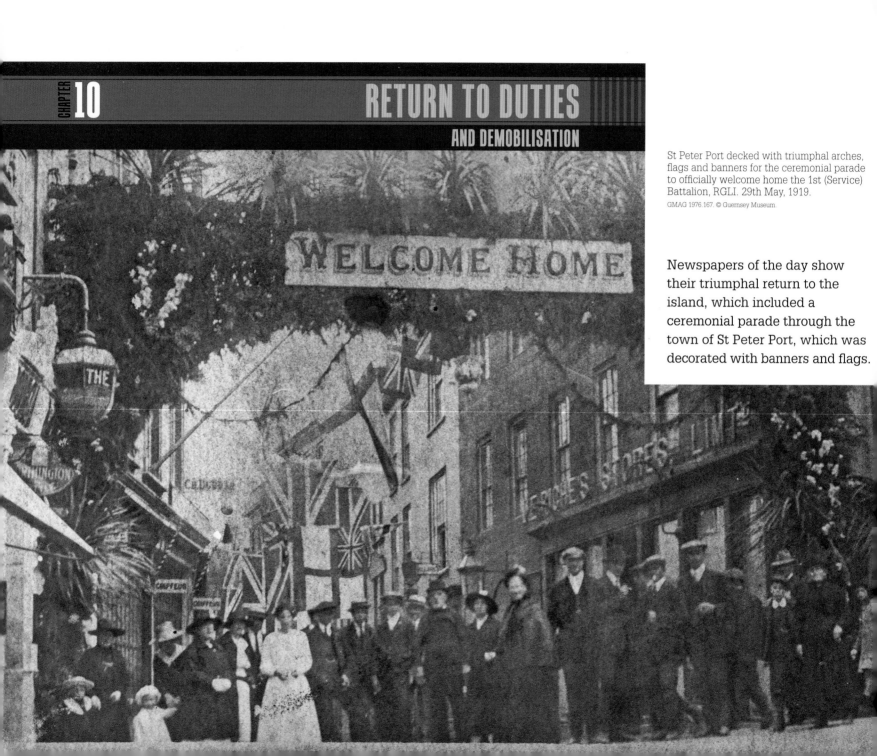

WELCOME HOME

St Peter Port decked with triumphal arches, flags and banners for the ceremonial parade to officially welcome home the 1st (Service) Battalion, RGLI. 29th May, 1919.
GMAG 1976.167. © Guernsey Museum.

Newspapers of the day show their triumphal return to the island, which included a ceremonial parade through the town of St Peter Port, which was decorated with banners and flags.

Some 200 members of the RGLI who had been attached to other units remained in France for some months more as the Details Battalion, helping to clear up the aftermath of war. RGLI Statistics in the back of a booklet entitled *Sarnia's Record in the Great War* [44], a copy of which is lodged in Guernsey's Priaulx Library state that the total number of men who served with the RGLI in the Great War was 3,549, of whom 2,430 were Guernseymen. By then end of the war, 230 had been killed in action or were missing, presumed dead. A further 97 died of wounds or of illness contracted whilst in service. 667 were wounded, and another 255 were taken prisoner of war. What it does not state is that many more died, sometimes years later, as a result of their wounds, gas or illnesses contracted while they were in a weakened state in Prisoner of War Camps. Private Le Poidevin was relatively lucky in that he came home to his family and was with them for many years after the war. Sadly despite having fought in the Great War for Civilisation, the War to end all Wars, he like many Guernseymen of his generation had to live under German occupation a mere twenty years later.

His brother Herbert was killed in action at Cambrai on the 26th of November 1917 and is commemorated on the Cambrai Memorial at Louverval in Northern France. The Memorial carries the name of 97 Guernseymen, and commemorates more than 7,000 servicemen of the United Kingdom and South Africa who died in the Battle of Cambrai in November and December 1917 and who have no known grave.

After he returned to Guernsey Latimer Le Poidevin wrote down his recollections of his time with the Royal Guernsey Light Infantry in a notebook, put it away and never mentioned it again. He remained on the island living an uneventful life, raising a family and working in horticulture until he and his family were forced to endure the German Occupation of Guernsey between June 1940 and May 1945. He survived this but died on the 22nd of January 1955 in England following hospital treatment there. His body was brought back to his island home and he is buried in Guernsey's Vale Independent Cemetery.

REFERENCES

INTRODUCTION

[1] Parks, E (1992) Diex Aix: God Help Us, The Guernseymen Who Marched Away 1914-1918, Guernsey Museum Monograph No. 4, Stroud, Glos., Alan Sutton Publishing.

[2] Parks, E. (1992), as above.

[3] Parks, E. (1992), as above.

CHAPTER 1

[4] Ford, D, Fear God and Honour the King. The Channel Islands and the Great War, http://www.jersey heritage.org/media/PDFs/ww1.pdf

[5] Parks, E. (1992) The Royal Guernsey Militia, Guernsey, La Societé Guernésiase, p.22.

[6] As iv above.

[7] The Manchester Guardian, 6th January, 1916.

[8] Ehmann, D and Marshall, M. (1976) The Constitution of Guernsey, Guernsey, The Toucan Press.

[9] Graham, J W, (1922) Conscription and Conscience: a history 1916-1919. - London: Allen and Unwin.

CHAPTER 2

[10] Davis, E.V., (1922) Sarnia's Record in the Great War, Guernsey Press.

[11] Acker, J.C., (1920) "Through the War with an Ammunition Train", http://www.archive.org/stream/thruwarwithourou00acke/thruwarwithourou00acke_djvu.txt

[12] Parks, E (1992) Diex Aix: God Help Us, The Guernseymen Who Marched Away 1914-1918, Guernsey Museum Monograph No. 4, Stroud, Glos., Alan Sutton Publishing.

CHAPTER 3

[13] Barnett, C. (1979), The Great War, London, Penguin.

CHAPTER 4

[14] Colloquial expression meaning not to panic.

[15] Several opinions, including "fear", "food" and "feed" have been given for the transcription of this word but it remains unclear. However Guernsey people often refer to having a feed of ormers, mackerel or other local produce when they mean a portion or a meal.

[16] http://www.firstworldwar.com/source/cambrai_hindenburg.htm

[17] Barnett, C.(1979), The Great War, London, Penguin.

[18] Slang term for Germans.

[19] An old Guernsey measure of distance.

[20] See Appendix 2, www.greatwarci.net

CHAPTER 5

[21] The underlining here reflects the notebook entry.

[22] Captain Harry EK Stranger, RGLI, won the Military Cross for his bravery in the battle of Cambrai. London Gazette Issue 30507, 1 February 1918.

[23] Horsfall, J, and Cave, N, (1998) Cambrai, The Right Hook, Barnsley, Pen and Sword Books.

[24] The Battalion casualty lists contain 491 entries for the period from 20 November to 1 December 1917. There were 20 casualties prior to that date. The discrepancy here may be due to the fact that men had become separated from their Regiment during the battle and gradually rejoined them later, as noted above. Some also died at a later date of wounds sustained in the battle.

[25] The London Gazette, 3rd Supplement, 18th July 1918.

CHAPTER 6

[26] The London Gazette, 4th February 1918.

[27] Parks, E (1992) Diex Aix: God Help Us, The Guernseymen Who Marched Away 1914-1918, Guernsey Museum Monograph No. 4, Stroud, Glos., Alan Sutton Publishing.

[28] Slang term for the Germans.

[29] Gillon, Stair (1925), The Story of the 29th Division: A Record of Gallant Deeds, London, Thomas Nelson.

[30] Parks, E (1992) Diex Aix: God Help Us, The Guernseymen Who Marched Away 1914-1918, Guernsey Museum Monograph No. 4, Stroud, Glos., Alan Sutton Publishing.

CHAPTER 8

[31] Slang term for being sent home wounded.

[32] The National Archives, WO95/3990.

[33] Where Private Le Poidevin was based.

[34] As above.

[35] The National Archives, WO95/3990.

[36] Imperial War Museum, Ministry of Information First World War Official Collection, item no. Q 1150.

CHAPTER 9

[37] Longpré-les-Corps-Saints.

[38] It has not been possible to identify the location of what appears to be Fant-Freres or Treres station. Transcription is difficult as the handwriting in the notebook is unclear here.

[39] Bourne, J. and Sheffield, G. (eds) (2005), Douglas Haig: War Diaries and letter, 1914 -1918,London, Orion.

[40] "G.S.O" (1920), G.H.Q (Montreuil-sur-Mer), London, Phillip Allen and Co.

[41] http://www.freefictionbooks.org/books/s/3988-the-sherwood-foresters-in-the-great-war-1914---191?, p.69

[42] http://www.gutenberg.org/files/32998/32998-8.txt

[43] The London Gazette, Issue 31840, p. 3833, 20th March 1920.

CHAPTER 10

[44] Sarnia is an old name for Guernsey. The booklet is a reprint of articles that had appeared earlier in the Guernsey Star newspaper, and was published some time in 1921. It is now in the Priaulx Library collection.

Barnett, C. (1979), **The Great War**, London, Penguin.

Bourne, J. and Sheffield, G. (eds) (2005), **Douglas Haig: War Diaries and Letters, 1914 -1918**, London, Orion.

Davis, E V(1921) **Sarnia's Record in the Great War**, Guernsey Press, (Priaulx Library Collection, Guernsey).

Gillon, Stair (1925), **The Story of the 29th Division: A Record of Gallant Deeds**, London, Thomas Nelson.

Graham, J W, (1922) **Conscription and Conscience: a History, 1916-1919.** – London, Allen and Unwin.

"G.S.O" (1920), **G.H.Q. (Montreuil-sur-Mer)**, London, Phillip Allen and Co.

Imperial War Museum, Ministry of Information First World War Official Collection.

Parks, E. (1992), **Diex Aix: God Help Us, The Guernseymen Who Marched Away 1914-1918**, Guernsey Museum Monograph No. 4, Stroud, Glos., Alan Sutton Publishing.

Parks, E. (1992) **The Royal Guernsey Militia**, Guernsey, La Societé Guernésiase.

The Official Diary of the Matron-in-Chief, British Expeditionary Force, National Archives Collection, Series WO95/3990.

Yapp, Sir A K, **The Romance of the Red Triangle**,http://www.gutenberg.org/files/32998/32998-8.txt

www.greatwarci.net

www.cwgc.org

Image courtesy of VisitGuernsey

FIND OUT MORE AT THESE CASTLE CORNET MUSEUMS

ROYAL GUERNSEY MILITIA MUSEUM
The story of the Royal Guernsey Militia is told with fascinating displays of restored uniforms, weapons and instruments.

RGLI MUSEUM
Follow the short but heroic story of the Royal Guernsey Light Infantry including a scene from the Battle of Cambrai, 1917.

Museums are open during normal castle opening times, please check the most up to date information at:

www.museums.gov.gg

Book produced by Guernsey Museums & Galleries

All images copyright as shown on captions.

Maps & images researched and compiled by **Matt Harvey BSc (Hons)**
Design: **Paul Le Tissier**   Illustrations: **Brian Byron**

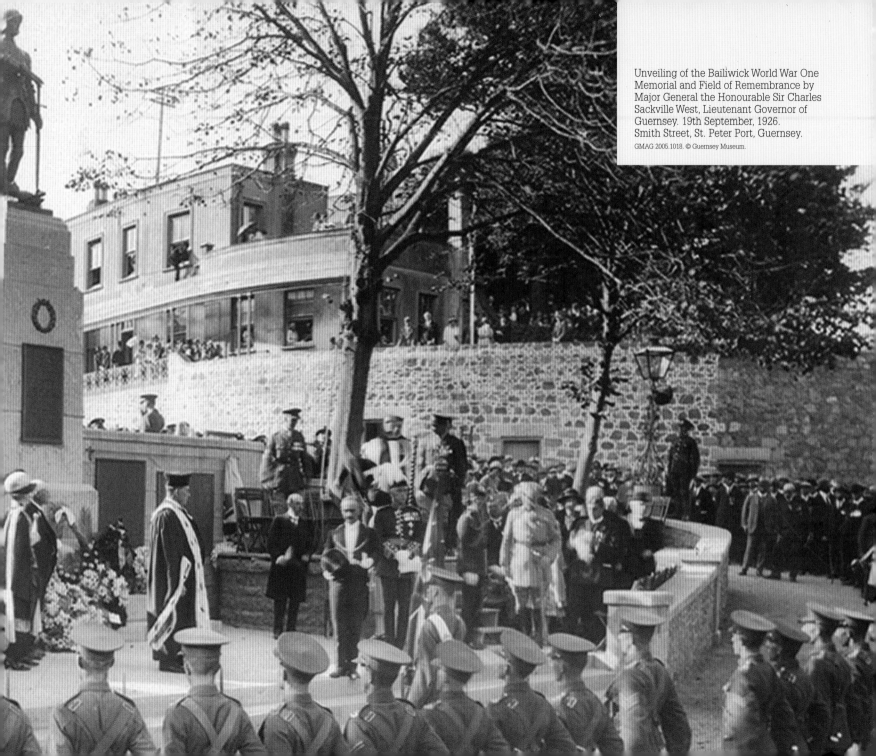

YPRES·1917

CAMBRAI·1917

ESTAIRES

PASSCHENDAELE

LYS

HAZEBROUCK

I

FRANCE·AND·FLANDERS·1917-18